CARLA DI FRANCESCO   MARCO BORELLA

FERRARA
the Estense City

Introduction
Paolo Portoghesi

Published by
ITALCARDS
bologna Italy

Foreword

What key can be offered today to the traveller who reaches Ferrara, attracted by an image, by now well consolidated in mass media, of an «intellectual» city full of literary pictorial and cinamatographic echoes; steady producer of a culture with unmistakable identity.

Ferrara is not «city of silence» any longer, but a typical Italian city of middling size rich in vital functions, a well-run city which for some years has been turning its attention to a very up-to-date problem of careful recovery of its own image, through the grandiose restoration of the walls and a programme of relaunching of urban functions. If it is true that, in the prospect of future, «small is beautiful» — since it can confront and solve its problems — Ferrara is an example of this revenge which small Italian capitals are taking towards moral and material capitals.

But Ferrara is not only this: an up-to-date community capable of programming a small resurrection is also the (τοπος) (topos) of a sense of space and time that has its seat only here, among the still waters of the Castle and the bastions penetrating them, among its «level streets as large as streams leading to infinity» and its façades proportioned in uneven rhythms, contradicting any possible identification between beauty and obviousness, among its corners riveted with pilaster strips, planted there to separate space and draw attention to this exquisitely «mental» operation, and the piramidal bases repeating even in small buildings the scarp-like foundations of the «metaphysical» castle, by now inseparable from De Chirico's image of the «Disquieting Muses».

Ferrara is a disquieting city itself in that it is rich in contradictions, «northern» as De Chirico defined it, but also warm and loving, attracted to the same extent by asceticism and refined pleasures.

In order to define the Ferrarese specificity, the character of Genius Loci in Cosmè Tura, Longhi writes of «immagination that flourishes on method and draws from it a ruthless coherence, sometimes an obsession».

Is it not the same «obsession» which is characteristic of Rossetti: to use only forms stic-ing to a simple theorem demonstrated once for a materials which stratify according to determin and unchanging laws.

Among all the aspects of the Genius Loci of F rara, the one on which it is better to fix our ey if we want to identify the «secret» of the city, probably what architects call «scale», t geometrical expression of a dimensional relatio The uman scale triumphs in Ferrara. Doors a windows are often cut exactly following the tra of the human body that goes through an openi or appears at a window-sill. But it would be puer to guess that this attention to the small scale resu from functional concerns or financial straits.

Ferrara knows the large scale of the Palace Diamonds, of the Palace of Ludovico il Moro, innumerable public and private buildings, but t way to the corner balcony of the Palace Diamonds is a tiny little door and in the pala the door leading to the balcony is much lower the the windows which circle it.

The human scale is a key which opens the l doors of Ferrara and characterizes an architectu that could be defined «of the listening silence «My ideal — Wittgenstein wrote in his 'diver thoughts' — is a certain coldness. A temple se ing as a background for passions without interf ing». The traveller may feel so much at home Ferrara and come back with pleasure among streets, because he feels that architecture is liste ing to him, because he finally finds himself front of a city which has moulded its own langua on pauses, one of the few Italian cites where t architectural «logos», the will of asserting and e alting, melts in the will of «legein» which is sa ing but also collecting and then, in a sens listening. Among so many logocratic cities, he in Ferrara is a city that leaves space with is silenc to that saying which for man is existing and a walking (De Chirico mentions the city «peripatetic friendship»), talking, feeling passio and confessing them in front of a backgrou which does not interfere and leaves us free but r alone.

PAOLO PORTOGHESI

A BRIEF HISTORY

Ferrara is first mentioned in documents dating to the 8th century A.D. They refer to a «ducatus ferrariae» or «duchy of Ferrara» that a certain Desiderius had pledged in 757 to Pope Stephen II. These records suggest that Ferrara was already a political and administrative reality by the Early Middle Ages. But let's look at the archaeological record, which takes us back even farther.

The earliest artifacts from the area date to the Bronze Age and were part of an inhabited site near Bondeno. The next settlement of any import was the Etruscan town at Spina, along the coast near Comacchio, which was founded in the 6th century B.C. and enjoyed a flourishing trade with Greece. In the following centuries, the area was to be ruled by the Gauls and then the Romans, who established settlements at Voghenza, Maiero and Gambulaga.

The «ducatus ferrariae» proper was founded along the main course of the Po at the point where the Primaro tributary branches off from the Volano. There is some controversy as to the original settlement that would develop into Ferrara. There are in effect two sites, and the archaeological record has been unable to establish which one was precedent.

One area lies between and near the confluence of the two branches; it was built around the Cathedral of San Giorgio, which bad become the new bishopric following the decline of Voghenza. The other, the so-called «castrum bizantino» (the San Pietro district) situated on the opposite northern bank, was originally a fortified military border camp.

Thereafter, the duchy came under the rule of the Langobards first and then the Church. In 986 Pope John XV awarded it to Thebald of Canossa. The city's outstandingly favourable position — situated on a major waterway, at a natural crossroads or hub between the all-important Adriatic Sea and the Po plain, and between Romagna and the regions to the north — and hence its strategic and commercial interest, made it the object of continual disputes between the empire and the papacy.

In this climate internal struggles arose between the more powerful families, divided along traditional lines into the Ghibellines and the Guelphs. But from the conflict there also emerged trends favouring the development of local city-based autonomy.

On the instigation of the Guelph faction, the Este family entered the fray and — thanks in part to assistance from the Venetians — soon became the city's most powerful family. They therefore took control of the city, and in 1264 Obizzo II was proclaimed Lord.

For over a century the rule of the Este family was marked l internal strife and disputes with the papacy. At the end of the fou teenth century, however, Nicolò II had the castle erected (1385) ar Alberto won from Pope Boniface IX the establishment of Ferra as a university seat (1391), providing evidence of a lasting consolid tion which was to make Ferrara a lively and famous city.

Niccolò III, Leonello and Borso all supplied further lustre to tl Signoria: Niccolò III by transferring the Ecumenical Council of 14: to Ferrara, Leonello by surrounding himself with a highly culture and refined humanistic, literary circle, and Borso by obtaining tl title of Duke of Modena and Reggio from the Emperor in 1452 ar that of Duke of Ferrara from the Pope in 1471.

In the meantime the city itself, the walled ring of which ha already been extended to include the walls of what are now Via Cavour and Corso Giovecca, under Ercole I (1471-1505) was fu ther fortified in grandiose style, extended and embellished with tl famous «Addizione Erculea» built by the court architect Biag Rossetti.

Alfonso I, Ercole II and Alfonso II were less fortunate in the rule of the duchy, finally losing it in 1597, since no legitimate he had been born.

The papacy then returned to exert its power directly over a te ritory that had been impoverished by the squandering pomp of tl Este family, and undermined commercially by the northward shi of the main course of the Po, which benefited the Venetian me chants. There began therefore a phase of severe civil and cultur stagnation.

Ferrara became a frontier province of the powerful Papal State the principal piece of work of the 17th century being the constru tion of the Fortress, demolished in 1859.

In 1796 the city came under French occupation and was later i corporated into the Cisalpine Republic, the Cispadane Republic an the Regno Italico before being re-annexed by the Papal State in 181:

With the plebiscite of 18 March 1860, the city became part (the Kingdom of Italy.

In more recent times the city was the scene of strikes organize by the labourers around the turn of the century. Particular remembered was the strike of Ponte Albersano in 1901, which ende in clashes with the armed forces and numerous casualties. Thes events bear witness to the determination of the peasants who fa< ed the land owners with a strong sense of political awareness.

Against this background the Fascists developed a strong follov ing in Ferrara under the leadership of Cesare Balbo.

During the last war members of the Resistance fought courageou ly, incurring heavy losses, while the city came under bombing raic during which a number of important buildings and monuments wer damaged or destroyed; after the war the citizens of Ferrara worl ed determinedly towards the democratic renewal of the Republi

HISTORICAL AND URBAN DEVELOPMENT OF FERRARA

Legend:

The old limit of the river Po

The byzantine castrum

The linear development of the town

The district called «borgo nuovo»

The district called «borgo di sotto»

The district called «Addizione di Borso»

The district called «Addizione Erculea»

The fortress area

The walls

THE CITY CENTRE

ESTE CASTLE

Its History. The «Castello Estense» in Ferrara is the monument most closely identified with the image of the city, and has played a role either as protagonist or as witness at every stage in the city's history.

Linked above all to the fate of the Este family, which obtained in 1264 by popular acclaim the signoria of the city in the person of Obizzo d'Este, the castle remained the seat of the family's power until their departure in 1598. Thereafter the castle was inhabited by the Cardinal Legates, representatives of the papal government of which Ferrara remained a domain until 1859. Today the castle is the property and seat of the Provincial Administration, and also houses the Prefecture.

Building began on the castle in 1385 following a violent popular revolt, triggered by the burden of taxation imposed by the Este rulers. During the uprising, the people had murdered Tommaso da Tortona, who was the Giudice dei Savi («Senior Advisor») and the tax adviser to the Marchese. The castle was designed to ensure the Este family secure protection and to constitute a centre of military power with which to control the city.

The Marchese Nicolò II commissioned the castle from the court architect Bartolino da Novara, an expert in military constructions (whose other works include the castles at Finale Emilia and Mantua). From 29 September 1385, the day that building started on the castle, it was called «Castello di San Michele».

The original plan incorporated an existing tower, that had already been fortified and surrounded by a moat. This «Torre dei Leoni», as it was named, formed part of the system of defence to the north of the city, ranged along the present-day Corso Giovecca and Viale Cavour.

Three other towers were built, forming a rectangle with the first tower, which was located at the north-east of the building. The towers were joined by blocks or «corps de logic» two stories high reinforced with avant-corps to defend the entrances. The castle was topped with battlements over the corbels (projections that jut out from the wall face).

To begin with, the building was used as a barracks for soldiers. From the second half of the fifteenth century onwards, under Borso and Ercole I, the building began to be used as an e

Castello Estense, *facing Largo Castello.*

nsion of the Marchese's residence, situated
wards the city square opposite the cathedral
d linked to the castle by a covered way, later
rned into a wing of the building.
Under Ercole II, duke from 1534 to 1559, the
stle was transformed into a court palace,
suming the architectural form that it has
day.

This transformation was entrusted to Girolamo da Carpi who demolished the merlons
and replaced them with stone balconies. He also
added another floor to the building and designed the «Loggia degli Aranci» (of the oranges)
on the first floor of the «Torre dei Leoni» and
the roofterraces on the towers. After his death,
the work was completed by Alberto Schiatti.

The Courtyard and the Interior. At the ground floor level one comes into the courtyard by way of the ravelins or half-moons and drawbridges. The Renaissance-style courtyard, to the east, stands out for its eight-arch brickwork gallery supported by stone columns, and by one cornice in stone and decorated brick, to which the original construction was joined, and a second cornice made of timber.

Two stonework wells of unknown origin are situated on two of the four rain-water tubs.

Near the «Torre dei Leoni», there are a series of rooms of considerable interest to visit.

The tower dungeons house the prisons that became famous in the events involving Ugo d'Este and Parisina Malatesta, the son and the young wife of Niccolò III, both decapitated in this castle on the charge of adultery, and Giulio and Ferrante d'Este, found guilty of plotting against their brother Alfonso I.

On the ground floor one may visit: the ravelin hall, an ancient entrance to the castle from the east, incorporated in the building following expansions made in the sixteenth century; the kit-

Castello Estense. 1. Facing Corso Martiri della Libertà; 2. Facing Viale Cavour; 3. Drawbridge of north ravelin; 4. Entry to the courtyard from north ravelin; 5. The moat.

chens area, with a low vaulted ceiling and lunettes, and with the traces left by brazier stands and cleaning runnels still visible on the floor; the cordon room revealing the outside wall of the ancient «Torre dei Leoni», with the typical stone cordon mouloung now part of the building.

11

There are several Renaissance-era staircases leading up to the piano nobile, but the most interesting way upstairs is via the ancient so called «cannon» ramp serving the fortified glacis. This ramp now emerges on the first floor inside one of the loggie designed by Carpi.

On the first floor there is a long series of halls all featuring painted ceilings.

These frescoes, commissioned in the second half of the sixteenth century by Duke Alfonso II, are the work of several different Ferrarese artists. Of these, the work of the Filippi family — the father Camillo, and his sons Cesare and above all Sebastiano known as «il Bastianino» — stands out.

In the Grand Hall (Salone) and the game room, the panels, surrounded with grotesque floral motifs, putti and imaginary animals, represent scenes of Greco-Roman inspiration depicting athletic games and exercises.

Castello Estense. *1. The courtyard (16th cent.); 2. The ramp of the guns (14th cent.); 3. Parisina's prison; 4. Hall of the Games, frescoed vault (16th cent.).*

Castello Estense: Hall of the Games. *1. Graeco-Roman wrestling; 2. The putting of the shot; 3. All-in wrestling; 4. The see-saw; 5. Exercises with the ball; 6. Quadriga racing; 7. The discus throw; 8. The hoop game; 9. The handball game; 10. Fighting; 11. Swimming.*

15

In the Sala dell'Aurora, the four phases of t
day are depicted with Chronos among the Fat
in the centre.

In the small Camerino dei Baccanali a
scenes depicting the triumph of Bacchus, t
grape-harvest, and the triumph of Ariadne.

The Chapel of Renata of France is perha
the first example of a place of worship of t
Calvinist confession, the religious persuasi
espoused by the Duchess, the wife of Ercole
Inlaid decorations with polychrome mar
tesserae make it impossible to set up any i
age whatsoever: the four evangelists repr
sented on the small vault were added in t
eighteenth century.

From che hanging garden, known as t
«garden of the oranges» or «of the Duchesse
overlooked by the small balcony of the cc
servatory (attributed with the small wall
Girolamo da Carpi), there is an exciting view
the square, of the cathedral and of the City H

Castello Estense. *1. Room of the Games: frescoed vault (1*
cent.); 2. Room of the Games: corner decoration with
tesques, festoons and putti; 3. Room of the Dawn: frescoed v
(16th cent.).

2

17

2

stello Estense: Room of the Bacchanalia. *1. Triumph of*
iadne. Fresco (16th cent.); 2. Frescoed fragment (16th cent.);
Frescoed fragment (16th cent.).
Chapel of Renata di Francia (16th cent.).

19

Castello Estense. *1. Hall of the escutcheons; 2. Hall of t
banquets, today Council Hall; 3. The duchesses' garden.*

2

CHURCH OF SAN GIULIANO

At the exit of the south ravelin of the cast
stands the small church of San Giuliano. Th
is a reconstruction (carried out in 1405)
another church which until 1385 stood on th
area on which the castle was then built, an
which therefore had to be demolished.

Built by Camerlengo Galeotto degli Avogadr
ad is recorded in Latin on a small stone, th
church of San Giuliano has a façade of co
siderable distinction both for its harmony an
for the finely modelled motifs in terra cotta tha
decorate it. On the Gothic portal there is a hig
relief representing «San Giuliano killing h
parents».

1. *The gardens of Piazza Castello.*
2. *S. Giuliano's Church (15th cent.)*
3. *The Town Hall facing the Cathedral and down Corso Ma
tiri della Libertà; in the background the towers of the Cast*
4. *Town Hall: the reconstruction of the Gothic façade.*

2

ALAZZO MUNICIPALE

he Exterior. It is but a short walk to Piazza
vonarola, with its statue to Girolamo
vonarola by Stefano Galletti (1875), and the
lazzo Municipale. On the way, we pass under
e arches connecting Este Castle with the Este
lazzo, which once boasted the famous
amerini di alabastro» or the private «alabaster
oms» of Duke Alfonso I.
The Palazzo Municipale or City Hall is actual-
situated to the south along the street leading
the Cathedral. Once the private residence of
e Estes, it features on the side facing the Piaz-
a Renaissance gallery, whereas the rest of
façade was rebuilt by architects Angelo and
rancesco Santini in 1738, shortly after the
construction by architect Tommaso Mattei of
rchbishop's Palace which overlooks it. The
ction of the Municipal Palace that faces the
thedral is a free reconstruction of the
urteenth-century façade, executed in 1924-28,
gether with the Tower of Victory, housing on
s ground floor Arrigo Minerbi's monument to
e W.W.I victory on the Piave.

The Horse's Vault». Opposite the main en-
ance to the cathedral is the entrance arch to
e City Hall, know as the Volto del Cavallo.

4

Alongside this vault stand the statues of Du
Borso enthroned and of Marchese Nicolò
seated astride a horse. Both statues are copi
(Giacomo Zilocchi - 1927) of the originals th
were destroyed by the French in 1796. T
equestrian monument, commissioned by t

Town Hall. *The Vault of the Horse from the courtyard;
Courtyard: grand staircase (15th cent.); 3. The courtyard a
the Tower of the Victory; 4. Duchesses' Boudoir (16th cen
5. Duchesses' Boudoir: detail (16th cent.); 6. Archiepisco,
Palace: façade (18th cent.).*

2

5

«Magistracy of the XII Sages» to commemorate the death of the Marchese, was the work of sculptors Nicolò Baroncelli, Antonio di Cristoforo and Domenico di Paris; it was first erected in 1451. The classical Roman arch on which it stands was built by Bartolomeo di Francesco after the design attributed to Leon Battista Alberti. The other monument, original-ly erected in 1453, was the work of Nicolò Baroncelli.

The Courtyard. Having passed under the arch one comes out into the Municipal Square, the ancient courtyard of the Palace. Here one should note the stone trefoil windws, the portal of the court chapel (which itself no longer stands), and the grand staircase of honour. The staircase, the work of architect Pietro Benvenuti, constructed in 1481, has a vaulted ceiling with a dome on the landing half way up, the whole structure being supported by fluted columns and large arches.

The Interior. Having climbed the staircase and entered the grand hall, one notices that the interior has undergone major transformation.

One then passes from the entrance hall into the Great Hall of the Plebiscite, where the annexation of the city of Ferrara by the Kingdom

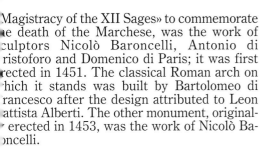

6

of Italy was decided in 1860. This «salone» features the outstanding work of Gaetano Previati entitled «The Horrors of War» (1894).

The only room that recalls the ducal residence is the «Stanzino delle Duchesse» (Duchesses' Chamber), constructed for Lucrezia and Eleonora D'Este between 1555 and 1560. Here one can admire a series of panels, divided by columns, resting on a wooden base; the decorations, grotesques, cupids, sirens, festoons, caryatids and divinities are attributed to Cesare, Camillo and above all Sebastiano Filippi.

THE CATHEDRAL

The cathedral of Ferrara dates from 1135, the year it was consecrated to Saint George.

Built in an austere Romanesque style, relieved by a pleasing symbiosis with the Gothic style, the cathedral is stylistically consistent with the most important religious buildings of that period (Cathedral of Modena, San Zeno, Verona, and others).

The new Cathedral, which eclipsed the importance of the old church of Saint George that is still found today on the south-east outskirts of the city, contributed in no small measure to the mediaeval core's expansion northward. About it there sprang up the most important publ[ic] palazzi, i.e. the residence of the Marquis, th[e] Palazzo della Ragione and the Palazzo d[el] Podestà, and the Piazza itself became th[e] centre of the town's commercial as well a[s] religious and political life.

On the façade, which is divided into three se[c]tors, the solid Romanesque style, with three e[n]trance doors, is apparent on the lower part, u[p] to the first balcony level.

After more than a century the round arche[s] were used to form three-mullioned window[s] with decorated rose windows, and the façad[e] was completed with a second tier of loggia[s] covered with other deeply splayed two-ligh[t] mullioned windows. The three tympana ar[e]

26

ompleted with a small-arched gallery and central rose-windows.

The tripartition of the façade is accentuated by the two pointed buttresses, while the central doorway is framed by a prothyrum (a single arch supported by two columns).

As is frequently the case with other works of that time, the cathedral's construction cannot be attributed to any single architect. The sculptural work, on the other hand, is attributable to Nicholaus, master of Romanesque sculpture, whose most eminent maestro was Wiligelmo. Nicholaus's name is in fact engraved on the lunette of the portal representig Saint George slaying the dragon.

The Cathedral; 2. The main portal. In the lunette, St. George and the dragon: bas-relief (12th cent.); 3. The porch. Lion with lamon: reproduction (19th cent.); 4. Right entrance with statue : Alberto d'Este; 5. The porch.
ext page: the side facing Piazza Trento e Trieste.

On the architrave, eight panels depict scenes from the birth of Christ, while the pendentives represent the figures of Saint John the Baptist, the Lamb of God, and a young boy bearing the book of the Gospel.

The prothyrum built in the mid - thirteenth century, is supported by lions and atlantes or telamones, eighteenth - century reproductions of the originals, which are kept in the cathedral atrium.

Between the two lateral mullioned windows of the prothyrum balcony stands a Madonna and Child sculpted by Cristoforo da Firenze in 1427.

In the tympanum there is a representation of the Last Judgement, inspired by the Apocalypse

27

of Saint John. By an unknown painter, this depicts at the bottom a procession of the damned on the right-hand side and of the blessed on the left-hand side, turned towards the large lateral lunettes that portray the fiery inferno and Abraham; at the apex a Christ in judgement encircled by the archangels, Saint John, and the Virgin Mary.

To the sides of the façade there are also a statue of Alberto d'Este, who in 1391 secured from Pope Boniface IX the bull for the university, and the bust of Clement VIII, who in 1598 came to Ferrara to restore the power of the Church over the city.

The north flank of the cathedral, skirting the Via degli Adelardi, preserves intact the Romanesque scheme. Divided into eighteen portions, each one is crowned with three small arches demarcating the balcony. It originally opened at its centre; this was the door of Judgement that led into the entrance to the cemetery.

At the far end of the cathedral one can see the semicircular apse, the work of Biagio Rossetti, added in 1498. This apse has high windows and terra cotta ornamentation which embellishes the overall appearance of the building.

The south sid has two sets of galleries. The lower one consists of twenty round arches supported by semicircular columns, each divid by three small arches on coupled pilasters. T upper gallery was added at a later period a takes the form of a long series of 65 sm arches arranged in groups of four.

Half-way along the south side there is cle evidence of the gap left by the demolition of t porta dei Mesi in 1717 to make room for t long arcade of the loggia «of the Merchant the construction of which had begun in the teenth century. The figures that decorated t door are now kept in the cathedral muse Another door, further eastward, known as t porta dello Staio, was also demolished for t same reason.

The campanile is also situated on the sar side. Building began in 1412 to a plan that h been attributed to the architect Leon Batti Alberti, but the work was never completed. T classic Roman style campanile, of sto throughout, contains in its first cube t fifteenth-century sculptures of the fo evangelists and, between the two arches, a br of Saint Maurillo in an attitude of blessir realized in 1466 by Matteo Castaldi.

The Interior. The interior of the cathedra the outcome of work carried out in the eig eenth century by the architect Francesco M

relli. In or around 1710 he transformed the
romanesque-Gothic five-nave scheme into a
nave and two aisles, locating the atrium in the
first bay.

In the atrium are preserved the original
mantles that supported the prothyrum, two sar-
cophagi, one dating from the fifth century and
the other from the fourteenth, as well as a
romanesque holy water stoup and a column-
bearing calf.

In the entrance are two frescoes, removed
from the demolished church of Saint Peter,
painted in 1530 by Benvenuto Tisi, known as
Garofalo. These depict Saint Peter and Saint
Paul. The two angels bearing the holy water
stoups date from 1745 and were made by the
Saccà brothers.

The most significant works in the right-hand
aisle include: a Madonna delle Grazie in the first
altar, a fifteenth century work attributed to Et-
tore Bonacossi; in the third altar, a Madonna
among the Clouds with saints Barbara and
Catherine, dating from the second half of the
sixteenth century by Bastianino; in the fourth
altar, a painting by Felice Torelli dating from
1735 and depicting the Martyrdom of Saint
Maurelio, with Saint Lawrence and Saint Francis at the sides, painting on wood made in the
mid sixteenth century by Ippolito Scarsella,
known as «lo Scarsellino», and a Saint Catherine
worshipping the Holy Trinity, also painted on
wood by Dielai at the end of the sixteenth century; in the seventh altar an altar-piece portraying the martyrdom of Saint Lawrence, a work
realized in 1629 by Giovanni Francesco Barbieri
from Cento, who was known as «il Guercino».
At the far end of the nave stands the monument of the Crucifix, with the bronze figures of
the crucified Christ, the Virgin Mary and Saint
John the Baptist. These works may be dated to
around 1450 and were executed by Nicolò and
Giovanni Baroncelli, who were collaborators of
Donatello. This group is complemented by the
statues of the city's copatrons, Saint George
and Saint Maurelio, created in 1466 by
Domenico di Paris. At the base stands the neo-

2

Renaissance funeral monument of Monsignor
Ruggero Bovelli (1955).

The niches on this side of the nave and the
corresponding niches on the other side contain
busts in polychrome terra cotta depicting Christ
and the Apostles, made by Alfonso Lombardi
between 1524 and 1525 for the church of San
Joseph in Bologna and transported to Ferrara
in 1771.

In the presbytery, on the left-hand side there
is the tomb of Pope Urban III, who died in Ferrara in 1187, and the bust of Pope Clement XI
is one the right.

The 150-stall wooden choir was built at the
beginning of the sixteenth century in the
workshop of Daniele and Bernardino Canozzi.
It is constructed in three rows in walnut, and
is decorated with marquetry depicting
monuments of Ferrara, deeds performed by the
Este family, and liturgical objects. The bishop's
seat by Luchino of France and Ludovico da
Brescia was carved in 1534.

The bowl-shaped vault of the apse contains
the splendid fresco of the Last Judgement
painted by «il Bastianino» between 1577 and
1580. This work was clearly inspired by the
similar Last Judgement that Michelangelo had
frescoed in the Sistine Chapel in Rome.

The apse stuccoes were made at the end of
the sixteenth century by Agostino Rossi and
Vincenzo Bagnoli.

From the far end of the left-hand aisle one can
enter the chapel of the Blessed Sacrament

Cathedral: interior. *1. Nave; 2. S*
Peter: Benvenuto Tisi (16th cent.);
St. Paul: Benvenuto Tisi (16th cent.
4. Angel with holy-water font: Vace
brothers (18th cent.).

lorned with an eighteenth century Last Sup-
er by Giacomo Parolini.

Returning along the left-hand aisle to the first
tar one encounters a Crowning of the Virgin
Iary, painted on wood in the sixteenth century
y Francesco Raibolini, who was known as «il
rancia».

The nave's central altar, in the fourth chapel,
ontains a canvas that depicts the martyrdom
 Saint George, an eighteenth century work ex-
cuted by Ercole Graziani; on the right-hand
de there is a depiction of the Betrothal of the
irgin Mary by Nicolò Roselli made at the end
 the sixteenth century, and on the left a Virgin
Iary as Intercessor, a sixteenth century oil on
ood, tentatively attributed to Benvenuto Tisi,
nown as «il Garofalo».

The sixth chapel features a Madonna on the
hrone with Saints, the work of «il Garofalo»
524).

In the last chapel stands a magnificent Byzan-
ne-era octagonal baptismal font, consisting of
 single piece of marble.

athedral: interior. *1. Choir and apse; 2. The 150 gilded-wood
alls of the choir (16th cent.); 3. Apse. Detail of Last Judge-
ent: fresco by Sebastiano Filippi (16th cent.).*

3

THE CATHEDRAL MUSEUM

The cathedral museum can be reached directly from the atrium.

The museum houses many interesting works. The following rapid survey mentions the pieces of greatest artistic value.

In the museum are kept the decorative panels of the organ that Cosimo Tura, the master of the Ferrarese school, executed in 1469. These altar-pieces, arranged in pairs, depict Saint George and the Princess, with the doors ope and the Annunciation, with the doors close

Of the sculptures, mention must be made a Madonna del Melograno, created in 1406 Jacopo della Quercia as well as a Saint Maureli made by the same sculptor in 1422.

There are also eight interesting lar tapestries by the Flemish artist Johannes Ka cher, made in Ferrara between 1551 and 155 following cartoons by Camillo Filippi.

The other lapidary works of considerable i terest include the panels of the thirteent century pulpit; a Romanesque twelfth-centu

pital in the style of Antelamo, depicting
erod, Salomè and John the Baptist; and, last-
, twelve panels, depicting allegories of the
onths, an equestrian statue of Guglielmo degli
delardi and a capital from the Porta dei Mesi,
t the Cathedral's south entrance, decorated
om 1226 onwards.

athedral Museum: organ piece. *1. St. George and the
rincess: Cosimo Tura (15th cent.); 2. Annunciation: Cosimo
ura (15th cent.)*.

GIACOMO DA SIENA 1408

athedral Museum. *1. St. Maurelius Bishop: Jacopo della*
uercia (15th cent.); 2. Madonna of the Ponegranate: Jacopo
lla Quercia (15th cent.); 3. Illuminated choral book: detail
5th cent.); 4. Beheading of St. Maurelius: detail of tapestry
6th cent.); 5. Acclamation of St. Maurelius Bishop: tapestry
6th cent.)

PIAZZA TRENTO E TRIESTE

Piazza Trento e Trieste is the market square built on the site where the walls that formerly encircled Ferrara were torn down in the ninth and tenth centuries.

Overlooking the square, facing the Loggia dei Merciai («Merchants' Gallery»), and alongside the cathedral, stands the Clock Tower. Originally constructed in the thirteenth century, the tower was renovated and raised in 1603 by Giovan Battista Aleotti. The modern edifice was built over the remains of the thirteenth-century Palazzo della Ragione. Of this building, destroyed after the Second World War, there remain a number of stone pilasters. Alongside stands the modern reconstruction of the thirteenth-century Torre dei Ribelli («Tower of Rebels»). On the shorter east side of the square stands the Palazzo di San Crispino, the ancient seat of the Shoemakers' Guildhall. The façade of this building, reconstructed in the mid-nineteenth century, closes off the Renaissance gallery that may be seen to the side of Via Mazzini, at the entrance to the ancient Jewish Ghetto.

Cathedral Museum. Door of the Months: panel with the month of September (12th cent.); 2. Piazza Trento e Trieste. View of the north side: the side of the Cathedral; 3. View of the south side: building built on the foundations of the Palazzo della Ragione.

CHURCH OF SAN ROMANO

One side of this church «leans», as it were, on Piazza Trento e Trieste, and overlooks the Via di San Romano.

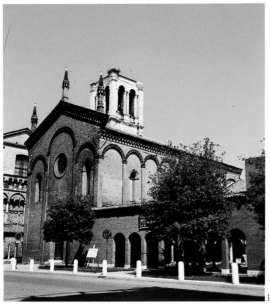

The original plan of the church dates back the tenth century. Later, however, it wa embellished, and the apse and small cloiste were added in the eleventh century, and fina ly, during the fourteenth century, the churc was completed, assuming its present-day forn

Both the thirteenth-century bas-relief in th lunette, depicting Saint Romanus on horsebac and the pre-Romanesque terracotta decoratio in the apse are of particular interest.

The hall-shaped church interior with its or apse is linked to a small sacristy. The fresc fragments belong to a series of frescoes remo ed from the church and now kept in th Pinacoteca Nazionale (National Picture gallery

The small cloister, rebuilt following damag suffered during the Second World War, has very pleasant and harmonious appearanc thanks to the sequence of small colum dominated by original capitals, the oldest which are tenth-century.

1. San Romano's Church; 2. San Romano's Cloister.

THE MEDIEVAL CITY

The old centre of Ferrara with its many
monuments and buildings of historic interest —
it is, the part of the city enclosed within the
naissance walls — is clearly divisible into two
tinct parts dating from different periods, each
th its own characteristics, separated geo-
aphically by the axis formed by Viale Cavour
nce the site of the Panfilio canal which linked
e castle moat to the nearby town of
ntelagoscuro) and Corso Giovecca. To the
uth of this line can be found the oldest part
the city, expanded in the 15th century as the
pulation grew; to the north lies the Re-
issance zone known as the «Ercole Addition»
er the town-planning project that made Ferra into the «first city of Europe», famous for
intelligent, far-sighted urban planning.

A brief consideration of the major stages in
e city's development in the Middle Ages and
e 15th century will help us to understand bet-
its layout; within the centre, in fact, a
mber of different zones can be recognized,
ch of which is characterized by a different
pe of street plan.

In broad terms the main phases of the city's
owth may be summarised thus:

1) The earliest settlement on the site of
esent-day Ferrara was a **castrum** or military
mp established by the Byzantines of Raven-
to defend their territory on the left bank of
e river near a ford. At that time (8th century)
e area was a lagoon and had already seen the
owth of a small town with a cathedral, the
esent-day San Giorgio, on the right bank of
e river. San Giorgio remained the cathedral
Ferrara until 1135. The Byzantine camp, also
own as the Cortesi castle, was situated in the
ea bound by the present Vie Ghisiglieri, Borgo
Sotto, Carmelino, Cammello and, to the
uth, Via Carlo Mayr, which follows the line
the left bank of the river Po Grande of the
ne. The main street of the castrum was the
esent-day Via Porta San Pietro.

2) As a result of its proximity to the ford the
ttlement soon became a trading as well as a
ilitary centre; to allow for the necessary ex-
nsion of the city canals were dug in order to
ain the land; in 984 Tedaldo of Canossa, the
w feudal lord of Ferrara, began the construc-
on of the Tedaldo Castle, situated west of the
strum on the same bank of the river
estroyed in the early 17th century to make
ay for the papal fortress); thus the **linear
yout** of this part of the city came into being
tween the two small fortresses linked to the

north by the defensive line of the first walls
which followed the line of the former Via dei
Sabbioni, the present-day Via Garibaldi, Via
Mazzini, Via Saraceno, and limited and protected to the south by the river.

In this period from the end of the tenth to the
twelfth centuries Ferrara was organized around
the three main axes which crossed the city from
west to east — Via Ripagrande — Via Carlo
Mayr acting as the quayside for the port, Via
delle Volte serving the trading activity which
came to the town from the port and Via dei Sabbioni; these were crossed in this period by the
Santo Stefano canal (today Via Bocca Canale di
Santo Stefano) which ran north-south across the
city, dividing it into two «islets».

3) After the foundation of the cathedral in 1135
a number of new streets sprung up around it:
Via San Romano, Corso Porta Reno, Via Vignatagliata and others which linked the centre
of commercial life and port activity (the river)
to the new centre of religious and civil life.
Despite internal struggles which divided the city
in this period — the result of the move from a
feudal regime to a system of communal government — the city enjoyed a certain prosperity
which had an important effect upon its urban
growth. As well as the development of the new
centre which saw the construction of the Palazzo della Ragione and the Palazzo del Signore,
later the Palazzo Ducale, completed in 1283,
there was a continual expansion northwards.

4) The area beyond the walls saw the
development of the **borgo nuovo** (new town),
with its centre on what is today Via Cairoli. At
the end of the 13th century the borgo nuovo was
joined to the city by the new line of walls which
ran along the present-day Corso Giovecca and
remained in use until the 16th century.

There is a certain controversy among historians as to the exact extent of the territory included in this expansion, known loosely as the
Adelard addition. The new line of walls included the area to the north of the earlier fortifications, some of which had already been
developed (the area around Via Cairoli, see
above) and other parts of which were developed
later, such as the area around the present-day
Via Voltapaletto and Via Savonarola, (once Via
di *San Francesco*), built up after the foundation
of the Estense Castle in 1385.

In this extensive district, bound to the west
by what is now Via Bersaglieri del Po and to
the east by Via Ugo Bassi and Via Madama, the
nobles of the Este court built their splendid

palaces with their large courtyards and gardens, many examples of which may still be seen in Via Savonarola.

5) Meanwhile, around 1320, the city had already embraced the district known as **borgo di sotto** (also called Borgo Vado), which had grown up around the church of Santa Maria in Vado; the urban layout of this area with its widely spaced network of streets crossing one another at right angles points to a later development than that of the earlier neighbouring district; this zone, which lies roughly between the Byzantine camp and the later city walls built by Alfonso I of the Este family and bound to the north by Via Cisterna del Follo, includes the delightful «Schifanoia» of the Este family (1385) and numerous religious houses which give it the character of an oasis of green within the mediaeval city.

6) Finally, the year 1451 saw the so-called **Borso Addition,** the connection to the city of the fluvial island of S. Antonio, rendered possible by the drying up of the Po in this area; Via Ripagrande turned from a quayside into a street, while Via della Ghiara (now Via XX Settembre), the link between the island and the mainland, became the line along which the new expansion centred. This new district was mainly inhabited by merchants and tradesmen linked to the land — slowly reclaimed by means of large-scale

drainage programmes — rather than to the a tivity of the port which had dwindled to nothi some time before as a result of the changes the river's course. Comparison of the urb layout with the oldest part of the centre sho even greater differences than in the case of t earlier additions: the main streets are broad a spacious and the houses, very different from t palaces of the earlier periods, were designed a more modern manner, though still retainir gardens and loggias.

The area to the south of Viale Cavour h undergone several changes in the zone now c cupied by the **Giardino district,** located b tween Corso Isonzo to the east and the city wa to the south and west. This site was original occupied by the Tedaldo castle, surrounded the Este period by houses, palaces and chu ches; on its margins there was the Belvede with the famous «Delizia» of Duke Alfonso. Th part of the city was demolished between 15! and 1610 to make way for the papal fortre which in turn was destroyed (almost obliter ted from history) in the second half of the 19 century.

To get an idea of the oldest part of the ci and of how it has developed within the conte: of the original street plan, the visitor must to Via delle Volte and its side-roads from V Lucchesi, Muzzina, Sacca, etc., to Via Si Romano, Via Ragno, Via Vignatagliata, V Cammello, Via Fondobanchetto, etc.; for an ir pression of Renaissance Ferrara, walk down V Savonarola, Via Terranuova, Via Paglia, V Beatrice d'Este and Via Madama. It is not o wish to press a particular itinerary on the visitc but to suggest that he walk through the: streets savouring their unity of texture ar power of suggestion. We do wish, however, draw particular attention to Via delle Volte, : named because of the vaulted walkways whic pass overhead linking the houses of V Ripagrande to storage buildings in the stre behind; the popular tone of the neighbourhoo together with its own particular charm, rend it one of the most famous streets in Ferrar;

This part of the city has a wealth of mon ments and buildings of historical interest whic are well worth visiting and which are presente in the following pages from west to east accc ding to the various historical zones as outline above.

1. Portico with Gothic arch in via Gioco del Pallone; 2. V delle Volte.

THE «LINEAR» CITY

From Via Garibaldi to Via Mazzini through Via delle Volte.

THE CHURCH OF SANTA MARIA NUOVA OR SAN BIAGIO

The church is noteworthy more for its antiquity than for its architectural value, its appearance having been marred by building works in the nineteenth and twentieth centuries. The church was founded in the 9th-10th century, though the site may have been inhabited as far back as the 7th century when it formed a small area of land above sea level. In the crypt may be seen the tombs of the Aldighieri, the Ferrara family from whom Dante took his name through his great-great-grandfather Cacciaguida.

mannerist style with its characteristic decorative display, it includes an impressive portal surmounted by the family's coat of arms and eight carved thophies and other stone figures. Formerly attributed erroneously to Aleotti (an architect whose work is quite different in conception), the work is in all likelihood that of Pirro Ligorio, a Neapolitan architect who worked in Rome with Girolamo da Carpi in the service of Cardinal Ippolito II d'Este and who worked on Palazzo Spada, to which the façade of our building would seem to be directly related. Ligorio's presence in Ferrara between 1568 and 1583 is, moreover, a matter of historical record.

PALAZZO BENTIVOGLIO

This edifice already existed in 1512, the year in which the Bentivoglio family took refuge in Ferrara after being driven out of Bologna, and was rebuilt in 1580 under Marquis Leonello.

Much of this splendid building, conceived on a vast scale, has now been lost as a result of vandalism of various kinds over the centuries. The façade, however, remains and is the only one of its kind in Ferrara. In typically Roman-

1. Piazza Lucchesi. Church of Santa Maria Nuova; 2. Via Garibaldi. Bentivoglio Palace; 3. Detail of the façade; 4. The portal.

SAN DOMENICO

The existing church of San Domenico dates back to 1726 and is the work of the architect Vincenzo Santini who decorated the restrained baroque façade with statues by the sculptor Andrea Ferreri.

Inside the church, the aisleless nave illuminated by the large windows is flanked by the side chapels with their paintings by 17th- and 18th-century artists from Ferrara (Scarsellino, Bononi, Cignaroli, etc.).

Among the more interesting works in the church is the small bas-relief of the Madonna and Child on the back of the high altar, the work of Antonio Rossellino. Also in the apse, the carved wooden choir dating from 1384 is a unique work of its kind in Ferrara.

Worthy of note are the sepulchral monuments of Gian Battista Canani, physician to Pope Julius II, Duke Alfonso II (1573) and Cardinal Giulio. These are to be found in the Canani chapel.

The church itself and the surrounding area were completely transformed by Santini who erected his work on the remains of a 13th century church. Of this latter today remain only an apse that serves as a sacristy and the mutilated bell-tower, both curiously juxtaposed to the façade.

Next to the façade of the mediaeval church (that is, the apse of the present church) once stood the «Crocette di san Domenico», the original seat of the faculties of science, humanities and medicine of the University of Ferrara.

Proceeding along Via Boccanale di Santo Stefano which, as we mentioned above, was in mediaeval times the most important canal in the city centre, we may note the colonnaded front of the buildings which give on to the street. Arcades of this kind are unusual in Ferrara, and were probably determined here by the presence of the canal.

In the line of buildings, **Casa Cini** stands out as a fine example of a type of architecture to be encountered frequently in the city; it is a mediaeval building with 15th- and 16th-century decoration.

Opposite this is the **church of Santo Stefano,** founded in the 13th century but rebuilt in the early years of the 15th. The façade with its bowed brickwork cornices (this type of decoration is very common in the churches of this period in the mediaeval centre) includes a rosette with a rayed monogram symbolic of Christ and medallions with the saints; the portal, which originally belonged to another church, is a late addition.

1. Via Spadari. St. Dominic's Church; 2. Interior: S. Vincenzo Ferreri resuscitates a dead woman: G.B. Cignaroli (18th cent.). 3. Interior: St. Dominic in Glory; 4. Via Boccanale Santo Stefano: Cini House (15th cent.); 5. St. Stephen's Church

2

THE CHURCH OF SAN PAOLO

Situated close to Via delle Volte, a thoroughfare of vital importance in mediaeval Ferrara, the church of San Paolo dates back to the 10th century. The present building owes its ex-

istence to Alberto Schiatti, who completely rebuilt it after the earthquake of 1570; work was completed in the early 1600's. The façade shows the happy fusion of local Renaissance motifs and the architectural style of the late 16th century with its Roman influences. The sober decoration of the interior, consisting of a nave and two aisles, together with the many paintings make the church almost into a gallery with a permanent exhibition of the works of late 16th-century Ferrara artists. Works by Scarsellino include the busts of the Carmelite saints located in the spandrels of the arches of the nave, a number of paintings in the third chapel on the left and, most importantly, the painting «Elijah taken up to heaven» in the vault of the apse. This work, which remained practically forgotten for centuries, has been re-evaluated by art historians and is now regarded as the unrecognized antecedent of the work of Carraccis. Dating from the last decade of the 1500's, it provides the first example of a religious painting in which the subject is almost swallowed up by its setting. This near reversal of subject and setting is so original for its time as to be almost tantamount to heresy.

The church also houses some late works by Bastianino in which can be seen the interweaving of his own style — the «Mannerism» of the

1. Corso Porta Reno: St. Paul's Church; 2. Interior. Resurrection: Sebastiano Filippi (16th cent.); 3. Apse concha. Ascension of Elias: Scarsellino (16th cent.); 4. Interior.

Numerous funerary monuments dedicated the memory of some of Ferrara's most illustrious sons are to be found in the church. many poets, musicians and painters are he commemorated that the church has even be described as the «pantheon» of the city.

To the left of the church rises the ancie **Leuti tower,** today the bell-tower. It is the o remaining example of the numerous towe erected by wealthy or influential families d ing the epoch of the Communes.

In former times there was a large monaste connected to the church, consisting of two cl sters, buildings and recreational areas whi once covered the whole site. Though rebu after the last war, the earlier of the two cloiste dating from the 16th century, is of great terest.

PALAZZO PARADISO

Tradition has it that this building derives name from a fresco painted by the artist Antor Alberti when Pope Eugene IV, the Emper John Paleologus and the Patriarch of Consta tinople, in Ferrara for the occasion of the Cou cil of Ferrara in 1438, were all guests of t house. The name, however, already exist before this time. Built for the Marquis Alber V d'Este in 1391, with the exception of a bri period near the beginning of its history it r mained in the possession of the Este family u til Cardinal Ippolito II sold it to the munici authorities in 1586 to provide the universi

school of Michelangelo — with the influence of Venetian painting in general and the works of Titian in particular. Amongst the examples of his work we may note the Resurrection, the Annunciation and the Circumcision. The large canvases portraying the story of Saint Paul on the walls of the presbytery are some of Domenico Mona's best works.

1. Leuti Tower: bell tower of St. Paul's Church; 2. Entra portal to the cloister (compound elements, 13th and 14th cer 3. St. Paul's Church: the cloister; 4. Via delle Scienze: Pa zo Paradiso.

th a single seat in the city. The change of use necessitated a series of alterations to the palace under the direction of Alessandro Balbi and Giovan Battista Aleotti. The most important of these was the construction of the façade on Via Scienze; previously the main entrance had been in Via Gioco del Pallone (the position of the old entrance, now bricked up, can still be made out in the wall). The new façade is characterized by its severe classicism, with strong emphasis given to the central section, this being heightened by the imposing stone portal with its double order and turret.

A further series of restoration and alteration work took place in the second half of the 18th century: to this period belong the present form of the entrance hall with its vaulted ceiling, the enclosure of the gallery above and the construction of the main staircase, the work of Antonio Foschini (1779).

Numerous alterations were subsequently carried out in the following decades by the University, which kept Palazzo Paradiso as its seat until as recently as 1963.

The restoration work now in progress will allow the Ariosto library, which has occupied the piano nobile since its foundation, to expand into to the rest of the building. During this work, begun in 1983, a considerable number of works of art dating from the most important periods

of the palace's history have come to light. In the room on the right as one enters the frescoes depicting scenes of courtly life, dating from the early 15th century, have been put back, while its partner (symmetrical to it in relation to the entrance hall) is noteworthy for its wooden ceiling decorated at the end of the 16th century (as in the preceding room) and for the frescoes attributed to the atelier of the Filippis.

Still on the ground floor, the former gallery, corresponding to the original entrance of 1391, is decorated with a wooden ceiling and monochrome frescoes belonging to the same period.

The anatomy lecture theatre on the ground floor has its own entrance and is the work of Francesco Mazzarelli. Built in 1731 to a classical pattern with tiers of wooden steps, it was designed to give students the opportunity of attending lessons in anatomy.

The floor above contains works from different periods. Passing through the first room (the former gallery, converted in the late 18th century, with its 15th-century frescoes unfortunately in bad repair) one reaches the 19th-century room with its decorated ceiling by Migliari and then another room with a late eighteenth-century ceiling and, on the walls, fragments of decorations dating from the 15th, 16th and 17th centuries.

Among the remaining rooms belonging to the last alterations of the palace the visitor should not miss the Ariosto room with the poet's tomb (brought from the church of San Benedetto in 1801). Beside the sepulchral monument, the work of Aleotti, the cupboards contain various relics of the poet.

The presence of the Ariosto library since 1753 has made the building one of the most important centres of culture in the city. The library contains over 200,000 volumes, incunabula, illuminated codexes and manuscripts, including numerous examples of work by poets connected with Renaissance Ferrara (Ariosto, Tasso, Guarini, etc.).

Palazzo Paradiso stands in the centre of one of the most interesting zones of the mediaeval city from a historical-environmental point of view: the streets — Via del Paradiso, Via Romiti, Via Carbone — contain houses and churches which, while not of any outstanding architectural interest of themselves, together combine to form an unspoilt whole of great beauty. For an idea of the atmosphere of this quarter walk down Via Gioco del Pallone — note the **house of the Ariosto family** at the corner of Via Granchio — and Via Cammello which follows the line of the western edge of the area occupied by the Byzantine castrum. In Via Cammello note the little church of **San Gregorio** with its typical 15th-century façade and, proceeding north towards Via Saraceno, the **house of Stella Tolomei,** called the Assassin, the woman who bore Nicolò III d'Este three sons — Ugo, Leonello und Borso.

Our visit to the «linear city» ends in Via Mazzini (part of the old Via dei Sabbioni, the north-

ern edge of the mediaeval city). This road w the nerve centre of the **Ghetto,** the area of t city to which the Jews of Ferrara were confi ed from 1624 to 1847; fronting on to the stre one may see the Synagogue, given to the co munity in 1485 and subsequently decorated a embellished inside. Also worthy of note is t group of houses dating back to the first half the 15th century with their typical high, narr façades with corbelled cornices and the pointed window arches.

1. Via Mazzini; 2. Typical medieval street; 3. Via Gioco Pallone. Houses of the Ariosti; 4. Palazzo Trotti; 5. Pala Bevilacqua-Costabili

1

HE «ADELARD DDITION»

HE BORGO NUOVO

The original 13th-century buildings of the rgo Nuovo have disappeared on Via Cairoli. e visitor may see, however, the Palazzo zzarelli-Crema which, erected in the mid-eenth century, employs the so-called «bald-che» (arches supporting the upper floor), here be seen in the courtyard; a similar construc-n technique may also be noted in the Casa mei dating from the same period. Fragments the original 15th-century frescoes which aped destruction during extensive alterations the mid-nineteenth century may still be seen; present façade, the staircase and some of decorated rooms on the upper floor date m the 19th century.

Not far away, behind the portal with the bust Duke Ercole II (traditionally ascribed to rolamo da Carpi), lies **Palazzo Trotti** which, til the middle of this century, housed the minary. Inside the building may still be seen o rooms with ceilings decorated by Garofalo the second decade of the 1500's, though un-rtunately these were extensively mutilated not any years ago.

IA DI SAN FRANCESCO

(**Voltapaletto - Savonarola**) This street as the main thoroughfare of the «nobles' arter» which grew up after the building of the

Castello Estense and offers the visitors a homogeneous picture with the many fine buildings — palaces and churches — standing side by side in complete harmony.

Note particularly the magnificently ornate façade of the **Palazzo Bevilacqua-Costabili**, which catches the eye with its trophies, busts and mottos in stone and brickwork. The similarity to the façade of the Palazzo Bentivoglio (built about thirty years earlier) is quite clear, but here the relation between the decoration and the architectural structure in less mature. The impressive effect of the foreshortened façade, however, is none the less, dominating as it does the surrounding fabric without actually overwhelming it.

SAN FRANCESCO

The church of San Francesco, work on which was begun over earlier Franciscan buildings in 1494, offers us one of the finest and most typical examples of the poetical architecture of Biagio Rossetti, whose inspiration remained unspoil-ed by the partial repairs necessitated by the earth-quake of 1570.

Both the exterior and the interior of the church bear witness to Rossetti's debt to the style of the early Tuscan Renaissance which, in his own personal manner, he reinterpreted in the light of his local experience.

On the exterior both the façade and the south wall follow the lines of the interior with their high lesenes. Note, in the wall, the position of

the large windows which, set low down, mark off the lesenes in pairs, the latter indicating the position of the side walls of the chapels; the interior was, as we shall see, greatly influenced by this arrangement. The great volutes of the façade, on the other hand, recall the composite orders of the Renaissance, particularly examples such as Alberti's Santa Maria Novella.

The brickwork cornice that embraces these two sides includes an unusual frieze consisting of tondi supported by angels who flank the bust of Saint Francis; the fact that this work is attributed to Domenico di Paris or to Gabriele Frisoni bears witness to the high quality of its decoration.

The majestic interior of the church is one of the earliest examples in Ferrara of the application of the compositional theories of the Renaissance — those or Brunelleschi in particular — based upon the use of simple geometric forms arranged in careful proportion: note especially how in the nave the square area covered by the central cupolas is balanced by two in the side aisles and two chapels. This strictly geometric layout does not continue into the transept, where the central cupola is flanked by two oval cupolas, or into the apse, which is broader than the nave.

Zevi has drawn attention to the manner in which the layout of the windows in the side chapels, mentioned above, illuminates the seven transverse walls which direct the light upward

into the aisles, giving the interior a unique «terrestrial quality» of immanence.

Among the many frescoes those by Girolam da Carpi in the nave and the transept stand o particularly; painted in around 1530, they po tray figures of saints surrounded by mon chrome decoration with leaves, putti an emblems. The decoration of the cupolas (whic have been reconstructed and reduced in heigh dates from the last century.

Inside the church there are many works of a dating mainly from the 1500's and 1600's, b unfortunately many paintings by famous artis such as Dosso Dossi and Cosmé Tura have bee removed; the works of Garofalo were taken the Art Gallery in the nineteenth century ar replaced with copies.

Works of particular interest include: th mausoleum of Ghiron Francesco Villa, a bar que monument to the condottiere who died 1670, located in the right transept; the inscri tion on the base and the bas-reliefs record th valour and courage of Villa, who led the troo of France, of Venice and of Savoy.

In the presbytery, the triptych by Domenic Mona showing the Ascension, the Depositic and the Resurrection of Crist (ca. 1500).

In the left transept, a sarcophagus in the sty of Ravenna (5th century), rediscovered in 192 on the site of the friary. It was used in th Renaissance as a sarcophagus for Francesc Ariosto, uncle of the famous poet.

56

3

*St. Francis's Church; 2. Interior: image of the Saint. Fresco
(16th cent.); 3. The Scourging. Stucco and fresco (15th and
16th cent.); 4. Mausoleum of Ghiron Francesco Villa.*

4

57

St. Francis's Church: interior. *1. Tryptych: Deposition, Ascension and Resurrection: Domenico Mona; 2. Shrine (17th century); 3. Jesus captured in the Garden: Garofalo (1524); 4. Pala Estense San Francesco.*

HE ESTENSE PALACE

(Also known as «di Renata di Francia»).
ow the seat of the University of Ferrara, work
the Palazzo Estense was begun for the Duke
1475, probably under the direction of Pietro
nvenuto degli Ordini; a few years later Biagio
ossetti was also involved in the project. It is
t possible to identify the hand of the latter

aster whose part in the work was very limited.
he original aspect of the bulding has in any
se all but disappeared (with the exception of
e low gallery of the courtyard) as a result of
terations commissioned in the mid-18th cen-
ry by Marquis Sigismondo Gavassini who
ught the palace in 1738.
The alterations, carried out by Girolamo del
ozzo, concerned the façade, the stairs with
eir stucco decoration and the rooms of the
ano nobile with their ornate ceilings (the work
Vittorio Bigari). The vast park enclosed by
e high wall which surrounds it has maintain-
l the overall shape of the old garden, albeit
ith different designs and layout.
The history of Palazzo Estense is closely link-
l with that of the Este family: given by Duke
rcole I to his Chamberlain Giulio Tassoni, it
turned to the family in the person of Ferrante,
en passing to the Cardinals Ippolito II and
uigi. The building owes its fame, however, to
enata di Francia, wife of Ercole II, who lived
re after she had been effectively banished
om the Castle because of her Calvinist beliefs.

CASA ROMEI

The house of Giovanni Romei, rich banker
and husband of Polissena d'Este, was built in
around 1445, probably by the ducal architect
Pietro Benvenuto degli Ordini.

Upon Giovanni's death the house passed into
the possession of the Poor Clares of the
neigh bouring convent of Corpus Domini. The
sisters used it for the occasional visits of illustrious guests such as Lucrezia Borgia, then
Duchess of Ferrara, and the famous Cardinal Ippolito II.

In 1870 the Casa Romei, in an extremely bad
state of repair, passed into the ownership of the
state. After considerable restoration, in 1952 the
building became the permanent home of the
municipal collection of frescoes and statues col-
lected from the various buildings of the city.

The building as it is today differs little from
the original Renaissance conception, there having been no significant alterations to the fabric,
decorations or individual architectural elements;
it remains the only extant example of a 15th-
century nobleman's house in Ferrara, the other
buildings of the period having been either extensively altered in the course of the 18th and
19th centuries (Palazzo Muzzarelli-Crema, for
example) or demolished.

The historical importance of the building as
a testament to Renaissance architecture is mat-
ched by the beauty of its conception; note in particular the charm of the courtyard with its
asymmetric layout of open galleries and supporting arches. This is without doubt not only one
of the most beautiful but also one of the best
preserved corners of Ferrara.

It is interesting to note how different this central courtyard and the layout of the building are
from the mid-fifteenth century architecture of
other centres of the Renaissance in Italy. Bruno
Zevi, noting the persistence of the mediaeval
idiom in the architecture of Ferrara, draws attention to the «grotesquely expressive» effect
of the main courtyard of the Casa Romei. The
heavy appearance of the external façade is con-
tradicted by the vivacity of the courtyard, accentuated by the lively quality of the decoration
in the upper gallery; the frescoes portray the
arms of Giovanni Romei with a rampant dog
framed by blossoms; originally the design was
continued on the painted shutters.

The large open gallery at ground level
situated opposite the present entrance is also
frescoed with decorations divided into sections
by painted pilaster strips.

The large monogram in brickwork on the wall
above bearing the Christological symbol IHS is
a later addition dating from the time when the

...use formed part of the convent of Corpus ...omini.

The tour of the interior follows a clockwise ...nerary starting from the east side (the room ...the Sibyls and the room of the Prophets); the ...sitor then crosses the main gallery to reach ...e west side with the 16th-century room and ...e «lapidario» and the rooms of the upper floor.

...HE ROOM OF THE SIBYLS: the room is ...ominated by the large fireplace with its ...ickwork moulding bearing the arms of ...iovanni Romei, the only piece of its kind in ...errara; the name refers to the wall frescoes ...hich portray the sibyls bearing scrolls prophe-...ing the coming of the Saviour; they are at-...ibuted to Andrea di Pietro and Giovanni ...aleazzo, Lombard artists working in Ferrara ...ound the middle of the 15th century.

...HE ROOM OF THE PROPHETS: the frescoes on ...e walls (mid-15th century) depict figures of

the prophets and scrolls bearing Biblical and philosophical mottos.

THE SIXTEENTH CENTURY ROOM: the decorated fascia is attributed to Cesare Filippi; note the large stone fireplace and, on the opposite wall, the fresco depicting the Madonna and Child, a rare example in Ferrara of a work by Antonio Alberti, an artist whose pictures are mostly found in central Italy.

THE LAPIDARIO: the three rooms house a collection of lapidaries, architectural fragments, sepulchral monuments and brickwork and stone decorations from various sources dating from the 15th to the 19th centuries. Among the many exhibits note particularly: in the first room, various decorative fragments (door jambs, architraves, etc.) from the Carthusian Monastery (Certosa); also the sepulchral monument of Tommasino Gruamonte Estense, dating from the end of the 15th century and formerly in the church of Sant'Andrea; in the second room, the pulpit from the refectory of the Certosa (early 16th century), religious works and the remains (head and hand) of the statue of Napoleon Bonaparte that once stood in Piazza Ariostea on the site now occupied by the statue of Ariosto. The third room houses lapidaries of various

...omei House. *1. Courtyard of Honour; 2. Room of the Sibyls; Hall of Honour.*

origin, armorial bearings and the collection of brickwork decorations (cornices, archivolts, etc.) taken from the city's Renaissance buildings.

On the upper floor admire the brightness of the rooms, decorated in the mid-sixteenth century by artists of the Filippi atelier at the behest of Cardinal Ippolito II d'Este; the grotesque designs of the fasciae and the ceilings immediately bring to mind those of the Palazzina di Marfisa d'Este which, however, are far richer and more complex. These decorations are characterized by a certain moderation and restrained grace that make the profane subject matter more appropriate in light of the use to which the Casa Romei was put at that time.

Note the ceiling of the third room with the central painting depicting Tobias and the Angel, attributed to Bastianino, and the picture of David and Goliath in the centre of the fourth rooms, also by Bastianino. The next room, the hall of honour, has a frieze with eagles within which a fascia bears the motto of Cardinal Ippolito (ab insomni non custodita dracone) of uncertain meaning.

The last, small room with its panelled ceiling decorated with woodcuts is traditionally thought to have been Giovanni Romei's study.

These rooms house a collection of frescoes (13th to 16th century) taken from religious buildings no longer extant, sculptures and furniture; note particularly the following: in the se-

cond room, the statue of San Nicola da Tole tino and a high-relief depicting the Depositi of Christ by Alfonso Lombardi (early 16th ce tury) and other marble reliefs of the Lomba school; in the third room, frescoes of the scho of Antonio Alberti (first half of the 15th ce tury); the fourth room contains figures of t saints by an unknown master (early 16th ce tury) and an interesting example of late goth sculpture (Madonna and Child with Saint Pet and Saint Paul); the far wall of the main hall occupied by the splendid Crucifixion by artis of the Rimini school (circa 1350) while the oth frescoes are parts of a cycle by artists of t Rimini-Padana school depicting the Last Judg ment (late 14th century). In the next room t visitor may see the Ascension by Serafino d Serafini (1361).

Despite its double loggia, the second cou yard of the Casa Romei is less magnificent tha the first; at the foot of the stairway, under t southern loggia, stands the coat of arms of Ca dinal Ippolito; the main body of the buildir above has, on the upper floor, a number rooms with wooden partitions painted wi allegorical figures, dating from the first half the 16th century, discovered during restoratic work.

The gallery opposite, which overlooks V Savonarola, has retained some of the origin decoration wich once covered the building's e terior.

THE CHURCH OF CORPUS DOMINI AND THE ESTE FAMILY TOMBS

Until the end of the last century the convent Corpus Domini of the order of Saint Clare occupied the whole block between Vie Savonarola, Praisolo, Campofranco and Pergolato; as well as the cloisters, various buildings and kitchen gardens the convent also owned the Casa Romei.

The convent was much loved and beneficed by the Este family, many of whom expressed the desire to be buried there; also of interest is the person of Caterina Vegri, saint, poetess and mystic, who lived in the convent in the 15th century.

Of this great complex, the building of which was begun in the early 15th century, today only a small part remains; still used as an enclosed convent, the only part open to the public is the church and chancel.

Proceeding from the church — completely transformed in 1770 by Antonio Foschini — one reaches the cancel which housed the remains of some of the most famous members of the ducal family: the simple tombstones which replaced the original sepulchres after the latter had been destroyed by fire in 1665 recall, among others, the Marquises Nicolo III and Leonello, the Dukes Ercole I and his wife Eleonora of

Aragon, Alfonso I with his second wife Lucrezia Borgia, Ercole II, and Alfonso II with one of his wives, Lucrezia de' Medici. The tomb containing the remains of Nicolo III, Leonello, Ercole I with his sons Giulio and Ferrante and other members of the family was placed in its present position in 1960; originally the sepulchres lay in the church of Santa Maria degli Angeli but were lost when the church collapsed; when they came to light it was thought fitting to lay them beside the remains of other members of the Este family.

Also in via Savonarola note the **church of San Girolamo,** an interesting example of 18th-century architecture, and, at number 19, the house in which Girolamo Savonarola was born in 1452, note too the **Palazzo Contughi-Gulinelli** with its severe 16th-century appearance; the attribution of the building to Girolamo da Carpi is borne out by certain similarities of composition with the façade of Palazzo Naselli-Crispi, an early work of the master; the portal is by Alessandro Balbi.

THE «BORGO DI SOTTO»

The Borgo di Sotto is interesting both for its fine monuments and, in Via Madama and Via Borgo Vado in particular, for the overall impression it creates.

In Via Madama, opposite the high wall of the «Gesuati» house, the visitor may see **Palazzo**

1. Romei House: the marble collection. 2. Contughi-Golinelli Palace. 3. St. Jerome's Church: main portal.

Polo, one of the finest examples of sixteenth-century Ferrara architecture. The portal and the rusticated corners of the façade, its prominent horizontal string course, the upper windows with their tympana and other features all combine to define the style, various examples of which may be found in both the mediaeval areas of the city and in the «Ercole Addition».

Recent restoration work (the building is today used for the offices of the provincial education office) has revealed decorated ceilings dating from different periods (16th-19th centuries) and, most spectacularly, the splendid decorative work on the walls of the main hall depicting a series of nine muses. The high figurative quality and the «architectural» layout of the whole work, in which the figures are enclosed within mock-marble frames, suggest that it may be attributed to Girolamo da Carpi and Camillo Filippi.

SANTA MARIA IN VADO

One of the oldest and most venerated places of worship in Ferrara. It was on this site that a miracle occurred on Easter Sunday in the year 1171 when, during the celebration of the Mass, blood gushed from the Host, staining the vault;

at that time there was a heretical belief th denied the real presence of the body of Chr in the Eucharist, and the church has been sacr to the cult of Christ's Most Precious Blo ever since.

Work on the present basilica was begun 1495 at the wish of Ercole I d'Este; two nam have come down to us as being involved in t project — Ercole de' Roberti and Biagio Rosse — the latter being described in the documer as «Director of Works», and this has led to so controversy as to the actual roles of the tv men.

Modern art historians tend today to the beli that Rossetti was not merely the executor of t other's plans, particularly as analysis of t compositional process has revealed that t basilica has much in common with both earli works (San Francesco) and later works (S Benedetto) of the master.

In order to gain a true understanding Rossetti's work it must be borne in mind th after the earthquake of 1570 the roof of the ais was considerably raised, affecting not only t building's proportions but also the diffusion

---

1. Church of Santa Maria in Vado; 2. Interior.

On the ceiling of the nave can be seen Gi[u]
Cesare Cromer's «Presentation of Mary at [the]
Temple» and five paintings by Carlo Bon[o]
also by Bononi are the figures of the saints [be]
tween the arches and many of the paintings [in]
the presbytery: «The glorification of the na[me]
of God» in the bowl-shaped vault of the ap[se]
«The flight into Egypt» and «The dispute in [the]
temple» to the sides of the large windows, «T[he]
marriage at Cana» and «The Betrothal of [the]
Virgin» on the presbytery walls; still in [the]
presbytery, «The nativity of Christ», «T[he]
nativity of the Madonna» and, on the ceili[ng]
«The Assumption» are by Domenico Mon[a].

The large central ancona contains Cam[illo]
Filippi's «Annunciation» (1561); among [the]
works which decorate the altars of the ais[le]
(some of which are 19th-century copies [of]
originals today in the Art Gallery) note the «B[ap]
tism of Christ» by Bastianino (left aisle, b[ap]
tismal font).

In the right transept the visitor may see [the]
small temple of the Most Precious Blood, b[uilt]
in 1590 by Alessandro Balbi around the rema[ins]
of the vault stained with the miraculous blo[od]
and brought here in the 15th century.

From the church one enters the Sacristy w[ith]
its many fine paintings by Bononi, Scarsell[ino]
and others.

Turning left as one leaves the church into [the]
first cloister, reminiscent of Rossetti's style, [one]
gets some idea of the monastery.

light within it. The interior was enriched with
sumptuous decorations on the walls and baroque altars in the side chapels, while the nave,
originally intended as a copy of the layout of San
Francesco with a pattern of squares covered by
cupolas, had a flat ceiling from the beginning.

If for a moment, however, we imagine the
nave divided into three areas, the cupola over
the point where it is crossed by the transept, and
the walls bare, the resultant proportions give a
truly Rossettian space.

Let us now turn from this critique to the
church as it is today; a little on the dark side,
perhaps, but containing a wealth of fine works
of art by some of Ferrara's greatest 17th- and
18th-century painters.

Church of Santa Maria in Vado: Interior. *1. Ceiling ca*[nvas]
«Miracle of the Blood»: Carlo Bononi; 2. Ceiling canvas «C[on]
demnation of Heresy»: Carlo Bononi; 3. Madonna of Cos[tan]
tinople: Andrea Rizo (15th cent.); 4. Shrine of the Holiest Bl[ood]

HIC EST PRETIOSUS D.N. JESU CHRISTI SANGUIS QUI ANNO MCLXXI DIE PASCHATIS XXVIII MARTII INTER SACERDOTIS
MANUS MIRACULO PROSILIENS SUPERIOREM HUNC IN FORNICEM INHAESIT · ADMIRAMINI ADORATE GRATIAS DEO PERSOLVITE

2

ALAZZO SCHIFANOIA

The emblematic name «Schifanoia» («schivar
noia» or «away with boredom») goes back to
origins of the building, today the home of
Civic Museum of Ancient Art; the first part,
fact, was built at the wish of Alberto V d'Este
1385 as a Delizia or «folly» - a building in the
dst of the quiet of the gardens designed for
t and entertainment. Schifanoia is the only
maining example of the follies constructed by
Este family within the city walls, the others
having been demolished long ago.
After being made Lord of the city, Alberto
d the building extended in 1391 to make a
gle-storied edifice of considerable size (the
ginal building of 1385 consists of the ground
or part to the left of the renowned portal).
e addition of the upper part of the building,
oposed by Duke Borso, was the work of the
cal architect Pietro Benvenuto degli Ordini
d dates from 1465-1469.
n terms of its size the present building is not
ry different from what it must have been
en work was completed in 1469, but its ex-
nal appearance must have been completely
ferent. It is worth stopping for a moment to
ture the façade covered by a coloured mock-
arble fresco (traces of which remain on the
st wall, today forming part of the museum)
d crowned by painted merlons; the colours
uld have been bright and festive, forming an
al background for the theatrical perfor-
nces which, contemporary documents tell us,
re given in the open space before the
ilding.
The façade was completed by the portal, the
ly vertically conceived element in it, which
ovides a natural focal point for the eye and,
the same time, is finely decorated, the decora-
n being sometimes attributed to the design
Francesco del Cossa.
Borso's radical transformation of the building
o involved interior alterations and the rich,
w decorations, some of which may still be
en in the Hall of the Months and the Stucco
om.
A later extension by Biagio Rossetti in 1493
ded another seven metres to the east of the

building and unified its appearance with the addition of a grand cornice of Rennaissance style.
   Centuries of neglect have taken a heavy toll
on the building. Passing from Duke Alfonso I
to Francesco, Duke of Massalombarda, and
then to his daughter Marfisa, it was then let
from 1582 onwards and used for the most varied
and unsuitable purposes - even, in the 18th century as a tobacco factory. As a result the wall
decorations, including those of the «Hall of the
Months», disappeared under layers of plaster
and were only rediscovered in the middle of the
last century.
   The present entrance to the museum (1986)
is through the doorway set inappropriately into
the façade in 1885. As from the spring of 1987,
however, the main door will once more be used, giving access directly to the «Hall of the
Months» and thence, on the mezzanine, to the
wing of 1385, at present undergoing restoration.
   Access to the Hall of the Months via the hall
and the nineteenth-century staircase is quite
wrong with regard to the conception behind the
great sequence of pictures within; originally, in
fact, the door through which one entered (the
form of which is still visible) was in the north
wall, access to which was via a large external
staircase that collapsed in the 18th century.
This change is anything bus insignificant since
it upsets the logical sequence of the pictures,
each one of which is intimately linked to those
before and after it. Upon entering one should

urch of Santa Maria in Vado: Interior. *1. Saint Vault of
Holiest Blood; 2. Cana's Wedding: Carlo Bononi; 3. An-
nciation: Camillo Filippi (16th cent.). 4. Palazzo Schifanoia.*

The orchestration of the spaces and t⟩ figurative concept of the work, however, is t⟩ fruit of the members of the «officina ferraresє the school of painters of the 1400's, who createʼ in the «Hall of the Months» their masterpiec the painters involved included, amongst otheɾ Francesco del Cossa (1435-1478) and Ercole dʼ Roberti (1450-1496).

The south wall of the sequence is no longʼ visible, but in the east wall, on which Francesʼ del Cossa worked, we can enjoy scenes crowʼ ed with the depiction of persons and eveɲ against the exuberant background of nature all her glory.

The panels of the months are divided horizoʼ tally into three fasciae: the upper one depiɕ the triumphs of the pagan gods on their chariɕ with scenes and symbols appropriate to eaʼ one; the middle one shows the signs of t⟩ zodiac and their varios decans; the lower oɲ portrays scenes from the life of Duke Borso aɲ from country life.

At present the museum houses collectionʼ bronzes, ceramics, paintings, etc., includiɲ some works of great value; the rooms are oftє used for special exhibitions.

The Stucco Room, which may be found nє. to the Hall of the Months, is of particular i⟩ terest; the rich decorations on the wooden cє ing and on the walls are ascribed to Domeniʼ di Paris (second half of the 15th century).

The last room on the upper floor — Rosse ti's extension — contains a wall painted resemble coloured marbles which provides ◆ with a good idea of the original appearance the exterior of the building; discovered oɲ recently during restoration work on t⟩ museum, it owes its preservation to the extє sion of 1493 at which time it became an inte nal wall.

Attached to the museum of Schifanoia is t⟩ **Roman Lapidary,** recently reorganized in t⟩ former 15th-century church of Santa Liberɑ

therefore turn to the right to face the south wall, which begins the sequence with a perspective view (almost completely lost) and then the month of January. Proceeding along this south wall one can make out scenes of courtly life in the spaces flanking what was once the fireplace and then the month of February. This whole wall is visibly damaged to the extent that some parts are illegible.

The months of March, April and May are on the east wall; these are followed on the north wall by a picture of horsemen and then by the months of June and July; an architectural view precedes the months of August and September, themselves followed by another architectural panel. On the west wall, through which we entered, the months of October, November and December.

This, then, is a complex and carefully constructed work, the symbolic and cultural content of which is traditionally attributed to Pellegrino Prisciani, celebrated humanist of the Este court.

Palazzo Schifanoia: portal.

THE MONTH OF MARCH: in the upper sectiɕ the Triumph of Minerva, goddess of wisdoɾ between a group of sages and maidens inteʼ on her weaving and embroidery; in the cent the sign of Aries; in the lower fascia the Duʞ exercising justice; the architectural setting the scene with its protagonists, putti and fe toons is on a classical model typical of t⟩ humanistic culture of the time; beside this, t⟩ duke setting out on a hunt amidst horseme falcons and hounds; in a separate section a sceɲ depicting pruning.

THE MONTH OF APRIL: in the upper section the chariot of Venus drawn by swans; the symbolism of the relation between the triumphant goddess and the figure of Mars (war) kneeling before her in chains is clear; around them are groups of youths in amorous attitudes and the three graces against a background depicting nature bursting forth in which rabbits, symbol of fertility, are prominent. In the middle section Taurus, the bull, with its decans. At the bottom the Duke gives a coin to Scoccola, the jester, while the courtiers look on; the return from the hunt and the Palio of San Giorgio watched by the Duke, the judges and ladies at the window.

THE MONTH OF MAY: in the upper fascia i
Apollo in the chariot driven by Aurora; abov
him the nine muses, Pegasus, the spring o
Castalia, sparrow-hawks, Python's skin on
stool - elements relating to his divinity and t
his Temples; also a group of poets and an arra
of putti; in the central section the sign o
Gemini; at the bottom a horse and part of a reap
ing scene survive from when a door was set in
to the wall in the 18th century.

On the north wall the first section depicts a
group of horsemen; it is attributed to a painte
with a style very similar to that of Cosmé Tura

THE MONTH OF JUNE: at the top the triumph of Mercury, protector of trade, on a chariot drawn by eagles; the god is surrounded by merchants busy bargaining while to the left the wolf and the donkey, symbolic of trade are depicted; on the right Io turned into a heifer by Juno and Argus decapitated by Mercury. In the central fascia Cancer; in the lower section Borso goes in procession to receive a petition from a kneeling figure and, in the background, a scene of life in a town on a river. The artist who painted the month of June is traditionally known as «the master with the gaping eyes».

THE MONTH OF JULY: the upper fascia is dedicated to the triumph of Jupiter who shares his chariot, drawn by lions, with Cybele, goddess of the earth; beside them a group of priests, a wedding procession and the cross - section of a church with monks; the central section depicts Leo; the lower picture is dominated by a substantial piece of classically inspired architecture framing the duke and others, possibly ambassadors; on the right the duke with Knights, on the left hemp-working.

THE MONTH OF AUGUST: in the upper fascia Ceres in a chariot drawn by dragons surrounded by people working in the fields (on the left) and merchants (on the right); in the background a city and, at the side the rape of Proserpina and the desperation of her damsels. In the centre Virgo; in the lower fascia Borso receives ambassadors and then leaves for the hunt; in the background Renaissance buildings and, on the left, threshing. The artist of this month, close to Ercole de' Roberti in style, is known as «the master of Ercole».

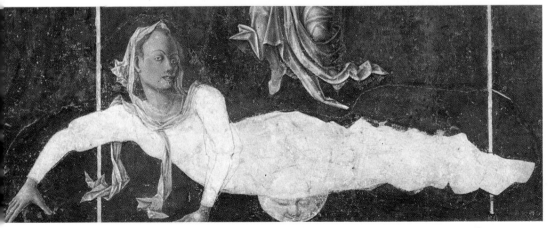

THE MONTH OF SEPTEMBER: the deity in the chariot drawn by monkeys is Vulcan, whose forge can be seen on the left; the shield depicting Romulus and Remus being suckled by the wolf is linked to the scene on the right, the Love of Mars and the nymph Ilia; in the central section Libra; and underneath scenes from the life of the duke: receiving ambassadors in an ornate building and on horseback with his retinue; meanwhile, harvesting in the fields. This panel and the architectural view that follows are attributed to Ercole de' Roberti.

ORATORIO DELL'ANNUNZIATA

Going down Via Borgo di Sotto the visitor passes in front of the **Oratorio dell'Annunziata,** also known as the Chiesa della Morte (Church of Death) as it was once the home of the Archconfraternity of Death (Arciconfraternita della Morte). In the simple architecture of Giovan Battista Aleotti, the church is best-known for the cycle of frescoes that make up the «legend of the Cross»; inside the panels decorated in the 17th century that link up the scenes, Sebastiano, Camillo and Cesare Filippi, Nicolò Rosselli and Dielai tell the story of the wood of the Holy Cross from the episode with Adam, on the point of death, from whose mouth the sapling from which the Cross will in time be fashioned springs forth, right up to its recovery by Saint Helena and the victory of Constantine over Maxentius. This cycle of frescoes is of great importance in the history of art in 16th-century Ferrara despite its rather bad state of repair, the result of later repainting and neglect.

As well as the cycle of frescoes there is a «Resurrection» by an unknown 15th-century artist in a style clearly inspired by the works of Pisanello.

ratory of the Annunciate. *1. Inner hall; 2. «Legend of the Cross»: Dying Adam. Fresco (15th cent.); 3. Resurrection. Fresco (15th cent.); 4. Deposition of Christ from the Cross (15th cent.); 5. «Legend of the Cross»: St. Helen's Discovery. Fresco (16th cent.); 6. «Legend of the Cross». Fresco (15th cent.).*

THE BORSO ADDITION

In this area of the city, urbanized in 1451, walk along Via XX Settembre, formerly Via Ghiara, the far end of which with its delightful **prospect** was added in 1776; more imposing is the similar addition at the end of Corso Giovecca: a main thoroughfare of the city, there was originally no gate at its end, and it was

Walking along the street we may stop to admire the façade of the house that **Biagio Rossetti** built as his home. Perts of the original building have unfootunately been last, but the

façade has remained almost a prototype of a style of house (not «palazzo») in Ferrara. The simple design, characterized by its coupled windows and brickwork decorations, was taken by Biagio Rossetti from Ferrara's architectural traditions.

PALAZZO DI LUDOVICO IL MORO

This grandiose edifice was long attributed t Bramante but evidence now available d monstrates that it was designed by Biag Rossetti, who worked on it from about 1495 t 1503, leaving it uncompleted. The attributio to Bramante was partly dependent on anoth error of fact which had the Palazzo built by A tonio Costabili, the Este ambassador in Mila on behalf of Ludovico il Moro; in actual fac however, the Milanese nobleman had alread found a suitable residence when he arrived i Ferrara, home town of his wife Beatrice, Duk Ercole I's daughter, after having been expel ed from his own town by the French.

Biagio Rossetti would certainly have bee

---

1. Via XX settembre: the Prospettiva (18th cent.); 2. Biag Rossetti's house; 3. Palace of Ludovico il Moro. External vie 4. Entry to the Museum; 5. Inner courtyard.

nsidered too modest an architect (he was seen
little more than a simple builder) to design
building of such a kind; in fact the building
bounds with features typical of his poetic ar-
itecture, a blend of Renaissance and motifs
ken from the local building tradition.
Over the centuries the Palazzo has changed
inds many times and undergone alterations to
oth the fabric and decorations alike; of the
ost extensive of these (18th century) today on-
a few isolated features remain. The small
ooms (next to the «Sala del Tesoro») access to
hich is via the second courtyard, are of par-
cular interest: recent restoration work has
turned them to their original elegance - the
ober stucco work, the painted ceilings and the
vo-colour terra cotta floors.
The building came into the state's hands in
)20; extensive restoration was carried out be-
veen 1932 and 1935 and it became the National
rchaeological Museum. During this restora-
on work a mistaken interpretation unfortunate-
reduced the loggia of the upper floor to a
egular series of open arches: up until that time
ie original arrangement of two open and two
osed arches had survived the various altera-
ons, albeit in a bad state of repair. This feature
the arrangement of the apertures in pairs —

4

was one that Biagio Rossetti used consistentl
in all his works (from his churches to his ow
house and it may be found in other parts of thi
building: in the south wall, for example, and i
the wall that gives on to Via Porta d'Amore
both of which also display his skill in avoidin
what is trite or banal by constantly varying bot
the shape and the position of the aperture
within the façade.

Note, in the unfinished courtyard, the ston
decorations attributed to Gabriele Frisoni an
the splendid brickwork cornice resembling tha
of the west side; opening off the loggia that run
between the courtyard and the garden, th
«Aula costabiliana» or «Sala del Tesoro» has
ceiling decorated by Benvenuto Tisi da Garofal
and assistants (1505-8). The scene with it
balustrades in perspective (the prototype fo
works of this kind was the «Sala degli Sposi
painted by Mantegna in Mantova around 1460
is filled with putti, people and animals set in
lively representation of courtly life; clums
restoration and reworking have unfortunatel
made it difficult to recognize the contributio
of the individual masters.

In the east wing of the Palazzo there are tw
ceilings by Garofalo depicting «scenes from th
life of Saint Joseph» and «Sibyls and Prophets»
both in a bad state of repair.

The area behind the building today offers a
e example of an Italian garden, including a
yrinth.
As we noted above, since 1935 the building
s housed the National Archaeological
useum of Spina with its collection of exhibits
m the archaeological digs on the site of the
ruscan city.
Spina was located in what is now the Valley
Comacchio and was,, in its heyday (6th - 3rd
nturies B.C.), a port and trading centre of
ormous importance through which all the traf-
between the Etruscan world and the eastern
editerranean passed.

tional Archaeological Museum of Spina. *1. Hall of the
ogues; 2. Internal hall; 3. Internal hall; 4. Red-figured pelike;
Red-figured kylix (ca 420 b. C.); 6. Bronze statuette represen-
g a warrior cutting off a curl (5th cent. b. C.).*

Because of its importance as a trading centre
Spina has yielded a surprising number of archaeological finds from Egypt, Greece and other
areas with which the city had links; in particular
the quantity and quality of Attic ceramics on
display in the museum make it an essential point
of reference for specialists and enthusiasts in
this area.

At present it is unfortunately impossible to
give further information with regard to the exhibits and their arrangement in the museum as
the major restoration programme now under
way will affect both the fabric of the building

and the organization of the museum. At the end of these works the museum will be extended into a number of additional rooms on the piano nobile: until then it is not possible to provide any further details.

National Archaeological Museum of Spina. *1. Red-figure pelike: Tryptolemus on winged chariot between Kore and Demetra (460 b.C.).*
2. S. Antonio in Polesine. External view.

ANT'ANTONIO
N POLESINE

Not far from Palazzo Ludovico il Moro is the rge complex of the Convent of Sant'Antonio Polesine, the entrance to which in Via del ambone is marked by a portal with a brickork statue of Sant'Antonio Abate.

Up until the very end of the last century the nvent boasted two cloisters with numerous her buildings, courtyards and kitchen-gardens closed by a high wall that guaranteed the closure of the Benedictine nuns. Subsequent poverishment and, in particular, the transforation of the western area into barracks have t, however, destroyed the magical atmosphe- of the interior in the rooms where the nuns ill live, in the cloister and, especially, in the rge unspoilt garden in the east of the complex. This is perhaps the only religious house in rrara in which as well as admiring the historic d artistic qualities of the building it is still ssible to sense the spiritual continuity that ks today's community to that of the past.

The nuns of the Benedictine order establish- themselves on this site (at that time an island) 1257 at the invitation of Beatrice II d'Este,

the daughter of Marquis Azzo Novello; Beatrice was also responsible for the enlargement and repair of an earlier Augustinian monastery.

In the centuries that followed the convent was the object of continual renovation and decoration, starting with Maestro Tigrino's work at the end of the 13th century during which the church and the cloister received their first frescoes.

Access to visitors is unfortunately limited to the outer church, the nuns' chancel and some of the rooms overlooking the cloister; the interest and beauty of the view from the little garden facing the porch of the outer church (15th century), however, make up for the limited access.

In the outer church the exuberant baroque decoration of Francesco Ferrari (late 17th century) stands out: the Eternal Father, the Madonna and Child and Saint Anthony and Saint Benedict are shown in the centre, surrounded by the Benedictine saints amid scenery set in illusionist perspectives; the stucco work that ornaments the windows and balustrades and the baroque altar complete the interior harmoniously.

The inner church or nuns' chancel consists of a room with three chapels containing frescoes

87

m various periods, mainly 14th century. This the most important collection of religious ntings in Ferrara, the 14th-century parts be-; of particular value. The chapel on the right ntains paintings depicting episodes from the e of Christ, attributed to masters of the Giot-school influenced by the Bolognese artists rly 14th century); the flight of steps that cuts ross the scenes was put in the 15th century allow the nuns direct access from their cells their church. The frescoes in the chapel on e left depict the stories of Christ and the rgin and were painted in successive stages by ists of the Bologna and Rimini schools. Under e ribbed vault of the central chapel with its

Grotesque decoration by masters of the Filippi atelier (16th century) we see: on the wall facing us the Annunciation attributed to Domenico Panetti (late 15th century) and, on the other walls, pictures of the Madonna and the Saints dating from the early 15th century.

The screen separating the nuns' chancel from the outer church has on it the Flagellation, attributed to Nicolò Roselli (16th century); the wooden choir dates from the 15th century.

From this chapel one may enter a small room with a decorated panelled ceiling on which one can admire the Funeral, a polychrome terracotta by Ludovico Castellani (C. 1450).

There are numerous other works of art in the convent: the cloister walls still bear traces of their 14 century frescoes; the chapter house has a fine wooden ceiling decorated with secular figures and grotesque motifs; the refectory, the «small dormitory» and other rooms reveal decorated fasciae and wooden ceilings from the 15th century, the period in which the first cloister of the convent was considerably extend-en and enlarged. Going out into the corridor one sees the tomb of the blessed Beatrice d'Este; outside, the beautiful arches of the 14th-century cloister; on the upper floor there are a number of small wooden columns which may date back to the original mid- 13th-century convent.

Antonio in Polesine. *1. Entrance portico; 2. Cloister; 3. ternal Church.*

ge 90 and 91. S. Antonio in Polesine. *1. External Church: ling; 2. Internal Church or choir of the nuns; 3. Choir.*

90

2

3

S. Antonio in Polesine. *Right chapel: stories of Jesus. 1. G* *ascends the Cross; 2. Jesus speaks to the Doctors; 3. Je* *descends to hell; 4. Crucifixion; 5. Crucifixion.*

94

ntonio in Polesine. *Left chapel: es of Christ and of the Virgin. 1. flight into Egypt; 2. The Massacre he Innocents; 3. Nativity; 4. osition.*

Antonio in Polesine. Central chapel: *1. Annunciation; 2.*
ght wall; 3. Right wall: Martyrdom of St. Stephen, detail;
Left wall: Madonna and Saints.

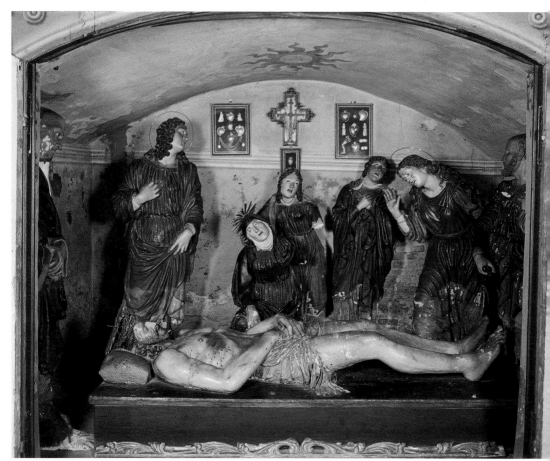

2

S. Antonio in Polesine. *1. Bewailing of the Body of Ch[rist],
polychrome terracotta by Ludovico Castellani (16th cen[t.)].*
2. Chapel of the Rosary: ceiling (17th cent.).
3. Aerial view of Corso Giovecca.
4. Municipal Theatre: interior.

ORSO GIOVECCA

This street is the dividing line between the [old]est part of the city and the sixteenth-century [ex]pansion.

[I]ts continuation leading away from the [Ca]stello Estense, the present-day Viale Cavour, [wa]s until the middle of the last century the Pan[ar]o canal, which ran between the two towns in [th]e west, dividing them; and, though this zone [is] mostly recent, Corso Giovecca still boasts [nu]merous buildings of high architectural merit. [O]n the corner near the castle we can admire [th]e impressive proportions of the **Teatro [Co]munale** (opera house), erected at the end [of] the 18th century by Antonio Foschini and [Co]simo Morelli; the decorations inside are by [19]th-century artists from Ferrara: Francesco [Mi]gliari, Domenichini and others. [O]n the opposite side of the street note the [Ch]urch of San Carlo, built between 1610 [an]d 1620, designed by Giovan Battista Aleotti, [an]d the 19th-century building that has replac[ed] part of the **Sant'Anna Hospital;** the civic [ho]spital, founded in the 15th century, was [situ]ated in the Basilian monastery, one of the [co]urtyards of which may still be admired in [Pi]azzetta Sant'Anna.

The hospital complex, which remained in use until 1912, owes its fame to Torquato Tasso who was shut away there because of his supposed madness from 1579 to 1586.

PALAZZO ROVERELLA

The attractive façade of the Palazzo Rover
stands almost opposite the Piazzetta dei Teat
the residence of Gaetano Magnanini, D
Alfonso I's private secretary, it was erectec
around 1508; it passed into the ownership of
Roverella family in the early 18th century ¿
was extensively restored in the 1920's.

Though there is no proof, the attributio
the building to the hand of Biagio Rossett
probably correct: the design of the façade
cludes a number of features often used by
Ferrarese architect such as the paired windc
round the lesenes (as in San Francesco), the ¡
tal and the rich decoration derived from lc
traditions.

Even more interesting than the individ
Rossettian features is the careful layout of

Church of San Carlo. *1. Façade; 2. Interior; 3. Dome.*
4. Roverella Palace. Façade; 5. Detail of the façade; 6.
court from the lobby.

6

façade: this is the only one of Rossetti's works viewed directly from the front and he here adopts an architectural framework that emphasizes the sense of space; the reference to Leon Battista Alberti's Palazzo Rucellai, the prototype of secular Renaissance architecture, is clear, but it is here reinterpreted in an individual, wholly «Ferrarese» manner.

Opposite this building, note the **Church of Santa Maria dei Teatini** by Luca Danesi (C. 1620), a fine example of the sober elegance of baroque architecture.

MARFISA D'ESTE'S VILLA

Further along the street, after the pleasant wall that encloses the university building, we find the villa of Marfisa d'Este.

The villa and the adjoining «loggia degli aranci» («orange gallery») are of great interest; originally they formed part of a larger complex of buildings and gardens in which lived Marfisa d'Este, daughter of Francesco d'Este and wife of Alderano Cybo, Marquis of Massa and Carrara.

The villa was constructed in around 1559 by an unknown architect and the interior decorated

by Camillo Filippi and his sons Sebastiano Bastianino) and Cesare; after Marfisa's dea[in 1608 the complex deteriorated rapidly unt after two cycles of restoration work (1910-191 and 1937-1938), it was rescued and opened the public.

Renovation work was carried out on both t] fabric of the building and the fine ceilings; the: latter were in such bad condition that in son cases Giuseppe Mazzolani, Enrico Gilberti an later, Augusto Pagliarini had not simply restore but to repaint them.

One example of this may be seen in the ba: quet hall where the extensive restoration wor

Church of Santa Maria dei Teatini. *1. General view of exterior; 2. Purification of the Virgin: Guercino (17th cen 3. Palazzina di Marfisa d'Este. Façade; 4. Interior: decorat detail; 5. Portrait of Marfisa.*

5

ough it follows Filippi's scheme, reveals the
ste and the hand of Pagliarini.
The Villa houses a small collection of objets
'art of mainly Venetian origin (furniture, paint-
gs, sculptures), assembled in around 1938 by
ino Barbantini.

Though this is not an exact reconstruction of
a Ferrara dwelling of the 16th century, but only
a collection of pieces (some of which are of great
value), the overall impression is a pleasant one.

The vaulted ceiling of the «loggia degli aranci», access to which is through the garden, is
decorated as an arbour with vine-shoots and
animals.

The street ends with an architectural
perspective that makes an attractative
backdrop. The 18th-century layout is by
Francesco Mazzarelli, while the side adjuncts
are of this century when the street itself was
widened.

*alazzina di Marfisa d'Este. 1. The garden; 2. Inner room.
The Prospettiva of Corso Giovecca.*

THE RENAISSANCE CITY

THE ADDIZIONE ERCULEA

As has already been stated, the city of Ferrara is centered around two areas which in morphological terms are quite distinct.

In approximately 1490, Duke Ercole I entrusted Biagio Rossetti with the task of enlarging the city of Ferrara. In its essentials, this was already accomplished by 1500: the city walls had been extended, the main streets had been traced, the first palaces and convents had been erected, the mediaeval walls to the north had been pulled down, and Via della Giovecca had been laid in their place. The new plan with its additions was dubbed the «Addizione Erculea».

Many different factors prompted the Duke to launch this undertaking, unique in the history of the Italian Renaissance states. Firstly, it was essential to defend a particular area, to the north of the city, which was already partially inhabited (the Carthusian monastery, the Delizia di Belfiore, and various other buildings were already in place), and which might otherwise all too easily be occupied by the Venetian enemy. Already, in the aftermath of the 1482-84 war,

the huge Rovigo possessions had had to be given up to the Venetians. Secondly, Ercole implementing a policy designed to encourag the influx of Jews, set out to create a populou and economically prosperous city, which woul accordingly require sufficient «living space Last but not least, the Duke was driven by th desire to turn the city of the Este family int a grand capital, supplying it with fine building and churches, i.e. an aristocratic district tha would bring him prestige and celebrity.

Rossetti embodied in architecture the Duke' resolve, creating a city which, though quite di ferent from the mediaeval core, is not so fa removed from it as is often a «rich district froma a «poor district». An essential point in thi respect is the fact that Biagio Rossetti did no build a city cut off from the previous one, as h might have done had he taken as models th contemporary theories regarding the «ideal c ty», which had to possess either a centric (syn metrical) plan, or at the very least a rectangula chess-board pattern. Nor did he seek to appl the theories of the treatise-writers, which woul have imposed a radial plan fanning out from th city's «hub», the Castle. Given the fact tha Rossetti must certainly have been aware of th

rk of the theorists of his time, and consider-
g his skill as a pragmatic builder, we have to
nclude that he consciously chose not to adopt
ext-book city plan. Although he had both the
lity and the means to do so, he evidently
eferred to view the city as an organism and
seek to match or suit the «new style» to the
d style» - the architectural traditions of which
had always respected.
This new Ferrara therefore featured an ir-
gular walled boundary, skirting around land
t the Duke had appropriated for the State in
90, and which was earmarked for develop-
nt. There are two principal axes at right
gles to one another: **Via degli Angeli** (now
led Corso Ercole I d'Este) linking the Castle
the nortern city gate; and **Via dei Prioni**
w known as Corso Porta Po, corso Biagio
ssetti, and Corso Porta Mare), running from
rta San Benedetto on the west to Porta San
ovanni on the east.
Along Via dei Prioni, there are two land-
rks that stand out: the Church of Saint
nedict towards the western end and the «piaz-
nuova» (now called Piazza Ariostea) towards
e eastern end. The square was designed to
eak up and lighten the city's north-south axis
ia degli Angeli), which, given that it led away

from the castle, from the outset inevitably had
to support the heaviest concentration of
buildings (it is of course no accident that the
homes of the most important personages of the
Este court were built along this street).
As regards the other streets of the «Ercole
Addition», it is worth noting the way in which,
as a result of Rossetti's city plan, they branch
off the Via della Giovecca towards the north in
perfect alignment with the earlier streets of the
Mediaeval core, thus creating a natural meeting-
point between the two parts of the city. Even
if not all of the streets were opened up by
Rossetti, it is obvious that his plan laid the foundations for the organic development of the
city, so that each successive step taken could
blend in harmoniously with Ercole's renovation.
Another of the plan's merits was that it was
drawn up with such «grandeur» that the area
enclosed within the walls was able to contain
the growth of the city right up until the 1950s.
Until that date there still remained large areas
of «green belt», once gardens and allotments,
an example of which may still be seen in the
splendid district surrounding the Carthusian
Charterhouse to the north-east of the city.
Lastly, a further point should be made for
those who are intrigued by this crucial
characteristic of Ferrara, and who would like
to find out more. If you follow any one of the
inner streets of the «Addition», chosen at ran-
dom, you will never arrive at anything that
might be considered a landmark, visible from

*Aerial view. The axis Giovecca-Cavour separates the
naissance city (to the right) from the medieval city (to the
); 2. Corso Ercole I d'Este.*

far off, inviting you to stop and rest for a moment. Rather you will always arrive at a crossing with another street or at a square, at which you are seemingly enjoined to proceed further in one of the several possible directions. This sensation can be experienced, for example, as one strolls down Via Frescobaldi or Via Mascheraio or Via Palestro, making for the highly attractive Piazza Ariostea.

The layout of the «Addition» is strikingly atypical for a Renaissance city (consider, by way of contrast, Sextus V's plan of Rome, structured around long straight lines marked at their beginnings and ends by obelisks and monuments). This atypicality enables the «Addition» to draw closer, as it were, to the older part of the city, while reminding us of the cultural background of Biagio Rossetti, a man of the Renaissance no doubt, but at the same time a discerning obsever of the past.

CORSO ERCOLE I D'ESTE

Anyone determined not to miss any of the charms of sixteenth-century Ferrara should examine the entire length of the principal axis of the «Ercole's Addition», the Corso Ercole I D'Este, from the Castle to the Porta degli Angeli. Numerous important buildings, parks, and gardens line this street. The final section, partially marred by more modern constructions, should be visited on foot in order to discover how the city gradually gives way to the countryside, which appears to enter the city from beyond the walls. It is an «abstract» phenomenon, almost unreal, but should be experienced.

Along the street the following buildings are worth noting: **Palazzo del Monte di Pietà.** Built following a design by Agapito Poggi and Domenico Santini around 1760, it features a huge courtyard, later covered over.

The elegant boundary wall and portal, at-

tributed to Biagio Rossetti, of the **Giglioli-V rano** palazzo.

The palazzo of **Giulio d'Este,** brother Duke Alfonso I, later the property of the I princes. This work too has been attributed Rossetti owing to the Renaissance façade, t way in which the spaces are drawn togeth towards the garden, and the care taken over t traditional Ferrarese terracotta decorations

Palazzo Camerini. Certainly one of F rara's most interesting eighteenth-centu buildings, in part owing to the interior deco tions: this building was erected by Antonio T in around 1830 to a plan drawn up by Pivid

The **crossroads «degli Angeli».** Whe the ancient Via Prioni and Via degli Ang meet. Bordering this road intersection, the stand four characteristic buildings whi however differ greatly in terms of both qual and size; this is a typically «Rossettian» tri designed to eliminate any possible sense of i mobility, using the different masses of t buildings to encourage the passer-by to cho between the various directions open to him

The **Palazzo Turchi di Bagno** (1493). A designed by Biagio Rossetti, it uses an auste pilaster strip to accentuate the corner only the simple surface of the building's facade.

Corso Ercole I d'Este. *1. Monte di Pietà (18th cent.).*
2. Portal of Giglioli-Varano Palace. 3. Giulio d'Este's Pala
4. Camerini Palace (19th cent.). 5. Turchi Di Bagno Pal
(15th cent.); Page 110 and 111 Palazzo dei Diamanti.

4

PALAZZO DEI DIAMANTI AND THE PINACOTECA NAZIONALE

The «Palace of Diamonds», situated on the south-west corner of the crossroads, is certainly the most singular and impressive building of «Ercole's Addition». Indeed, its marble shell is so striking and unusual as to make it unique in the architectural context of Ferrara.

Biagio Rossetti is traditionally credited with the design of the Palace, which was begun in 1493 by order of Sigismondo d'Este, a brother of Duke Ercole I. Building was interrupted in 1504 when Rossetti and his collaborator Gabriele Frisoni left the project, and was only completed in 1567. The Palace remained in the possession of the Este family even after their departure from Ferrara (1598), but was taken over by the Marquises of Villa who made a number of alterations, including the addition of a decorated portal.

The exterior owes its imposing appearance not only to the building's own expressive features but also to the architect's marked flair for city planning and perspective effects. The more than eight thousand five hundred ashlars of diamond-pointed rustication, seemingly all identical, are in fact arranged with great care so that the axes of their vertices are only

perpendicular to the façade across the midd in the top part of the façade, on the other ha the axes of the vertices are turned upwards, a at the base, the axes slope downward. T jutting-out of the «diamonds» and their sys matically «staggered» arrangement from c row to the next, gives the marble mass a v sculptural appearance. This effect is mitiga however by the way in which the building's c ner is, as it were, broken up by the sm balcony and the pilaster strips decorated Gabriele Frisoni.

The movement of the façade inherent in su an unusual facing is in this case carried over the dynamic function of its decorative who which is sensitive and intimately related to surroundings. This «relation» effect is typi of Rossetti's work, and may be found in ma other of his buildings.

The «Civic Gallery of Modern Art» is situa on the ground floor of the building. This gall holds periodic exhibitions of leading conte porary artists. The National Picture Gallery on the piano nobile.

The Picture Gallery (Pinacoteca), initia municipal only, was established in 1836 with purpose of recovering paintings that w

1. *Quadrivio degli Angeli.*
2. *Palazzo dei Diamanti. Portal.*
3. *Arcading on to the courtyard.*

noved from those city churches that were able to guarantee their preservation. Later acsitions, detached frescoes, bequests and gifts ve considerably enriched the collection of the llery, which gained national status in 1956. Today, as one walks through the exhibition ms, one is confronted with what is in effect istory of Ferrarese art from the thirteenth the eighteenth-century. Owing, however, to amount of material that has been lost over years, the great «Ferrarese atelier» of the eenth century is very poorly represented. To w this, apart from the circular paintings icting the stories of Saint Maurelio, it is best examine Schifanoia's Cycle of Months.

he exhibition rooms themselves have corated ceilings that are of considerable inest. These include the ceilings of the granse hall of honour, consisting of coffers nken panels), and those of the south wing h its central panels from the Convent of Saint thony in Polesine depicting a Madonna and ild and God the Father (fifteenth century). In three rooms following the grand hall in the rth wing, the ceilings have bands painted with ely and elegant grotesques dating from the d of he sixteenth century. The ceiling panels, w empty, once contained paintings by arsellino, Carracci and Cavazzoni: these were ved to Modena by the Este family before y gave the palace up to the Villa family 30).

n the way the Picture Gallery is currently arged, the entrance gallery with the portraits he Marquises of Villa leads into the main hall ere the large fresco of the Triumph of Saint gustine, attributed to the Modenese Serafino Serafini (second half of the fourteenth cen-y), is displayed. Also on show are the scoes (originating in the church of the Ab-y of Saint Bartholomew) representing the w Testament stories. Depictions of the angelists by an unknown thirteenth-century ist are also displayed: these make use of pular Benedictine and Bizantine- like motifs create an idiom that has no parallels in Italian nting create are idion of the period. Also in hall is exhibited the «Allegory of the Old and w Testament» by Garofalo.

he grand hall leads into three other large ms where the collection of paintings owned the Cassa di Risparmio (Savings Bank) of rrara is stored. There are roughly eighty rks altogether, including canvases, tablets d frescoes of local interest. These include rks by Garofalo, by Girolamo da Carpi, by stianino, by Scarsellino, by Carlo Bononi and other artists who marked the most signifi-nt stages in the development of the Ferrarese 1ool of painting.

In the series of halls flanking Corso Biagio Rossetti, works of the sixteenth-century Ferrarese school are permanently displayed: apart from the paintings of Vittore Carpaccio (Dormitio Virginis «Death of the Virgin», 1508) and of Ortolano, of Mazzolino, of Bononi, etc, the paintings in this section of the gallery are mostly the work of Garofalo — to whom the second room is wholly devoted — and of Battista and Dosso Dossi.

Of the works of Garofalo, special mention must be made of the «Slaughter of the Innocents» (1519), the «Finding of the True Cross» (1534) — showing the evident influence of Raphael and the Mannerists, combined with the vivid Venetian-School colours — and, lastly, the «Adoration of the Magi the» and « Nativity» (1513).

In the last hall, the large *Costabili Polyptych*, begun by Garofalo in 1530 and executed with the collaboration of Dosso Dossi, is on display. The Madonna with Child and Seven Saints, the

central altar-piece, encircled by pan depicting Saint A brose, Saint Augusti Saint Sebastian a Saint George, a above, Christ Res rected.

The Vendeghini-E di collection of Rena sance paintings is hibited in the so wing of the palaz which can be reacl directly from gallery.

Palazzo dei Diamanti. Pict Gallery. *1. North-wing with late - 16th - century ing; 2. Madonna and C (15th cent.), ceiling from S. tonio in Polesine; 3. Benver Tisi da Garofalo: Adoratio the Magi (16th cent.); Benvenuto Tisi da Garof Enthroned Madonna u Saints (16th cent.); 5. D Dossi: St. George and Dragon, detail of the Costa polyptych (16th cent.).*

2

114

5

115

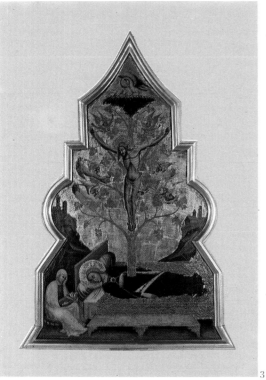

These paintings include works by Ercole
Roberti, Gentile da Fabriano, and Garofalo. F
ther on one can pause to admire the halls t
display fourteenth — and fifteenth — cent
paintings, including works by Cristoforo
Bologna, Simone dei Crocifissi, Vicino da F
rara, etc. Of these the most outstanding are t
circular paintings depicting the Judgement
Saint Maurelio and the Martyrdom of S
Maurelio from the saint's altar-piece in
Church of Saint George. Both paintings,
Cosmè Tura, reveal the high figurative a
spatial quality achieved by the «Ferrar
atelier» thanks to its great master. In the f
scene, the figures move within a strict persp
tive adorned and refined by pageboys and li
monkeys, recalling the elegance of life at
Este court. The drama of the second sc
presents us once again with the harsh and
hospitable landscape that is one of Tura's w
known characteristics.

PALAZZO PROSPERI-SACRATI

Situated opposite the «Palace of Diamonds», the Palazzo Prosperi Sacrati has been renowned ever since the sixteenth century above all for its portal. This stands out not only fot its position vis-à-vis the surrounding roads and buildings, affording a sense of dynamism to the *Crossroads of the Angels*, but also for its evidently Venetian-style composition and decorations.

Recent restoration work has recovered the portal's sophisticated use of the white-pink-grey colour scheme, and has made it possible once again to examine the friezes, decorated with intricate moulding patterns as well as its sculpted sections. Despite the damage and mutilation suffered during the war (in particular, the cupids and monkeys adorning the balcony balustrade were lost), the portal remains one of the most outstanding examples of Ferrarese architectural sculpture of the sixteenth century. Nineteenth-century artistic historiography deemed the portal to be the work of major artists, including even the Tuscan Baldassarre Peruzzi. Given the portal's typically Venetian aspect, the work might however be attributed, albeit with some uncertainty, to Antonio and Aurelio Solari-Lombardo.

Apart from the historical and artistic value the portal, the importance of its «positio which may confidently be ascribed to Bia Rossetti's genius for city-planning, should or again be emphasized. Rossetti, when it came designing the crossroads, instead of drawing a symmetrically organized plan, preferred polarise attention on two elements of particu expressive quality (the Palace of Diamonds w its balcony, and the Prosperi-Sacrati port which clearly emerge from the many soberlo ing, almost anonymous, buildings that surrou them. The deliberate dynamism of this comp tion, which achieves its effect by means of c trast and surprises, is quite apparent, ever somewhat mitigated by the corner balcony the Prosperi Sacrati building, a rather s indulgent nineteenth-century addition.

Further down Corso Ercole I d'Este following buildings are worth noting:

The **Trotti-Mosti Palace:** of great inter both for its architectural features, which typical of sixteenth-century Ferrara, and also the decorations dating from a variety of peri which have been recovered during the rec work of restoration. Particular mention must

---

ade of the Aula Magna, with its coffered ceiling and frescoed band, sixteenth-century decorated ceilings and Liberty decorations.

The **Guarini-Giordani Palace:** attributed ⹁ Alessandro Biondo, one of Rossetti's collaborators, this building has a front that was exnded «in style» in 1903. Together with Palaz⹁ Trotti-Mosti, it is today the University's Faculty of Law. From this point on the street is less and less built up. Further on, after enjoying the partial view of the Carthusian monastery from Piazzale Borso, one can walk along the stretch called Via dei Piopponi (literally: «Street of the Tall Poplars») given to the street form here to the Porta degli Angeli at the city walls.

THE CHURCH OF SAINT CHRISTOPHER AT THE CHARTERHOUSE

The Carthusian monks settled in 1461 in this area, which at that time was outside the city's walls. They did so at the behest of Duke Borso who commissioned Pietrobono Brasavola to build the monastery with the large cloister, which still stands. Not long after, while Ercole I was Duke, work began on the present church. The building was completed in 1551, though the façade remained bare. The portal was added in the late eighteenth century.

The attribution of the church to Biagio Rossetti, although not backed by any documentary evidence, is on historical and stylistic grounds convincing, even if the overall appearance of the building varies so markedly from that of his earlier works (San Francesco, Santa Maria in Vado, San Benedetto). On this particular occasion, Rossetti made use of a wholly experimental plan, entailing a single nave with side chapels. He presumably derived inspiration for this design from Leon Battista Alberti, and especialy from his work in Mantua. The organisation of the design into quadrangular domed modules reproduced in the transept and the chancel, and also the proportional relation with the chapels, indicate that the planning approach is the same, even if it is implemented here on a different kind of layout.

The technique for distributing natural light already used by Rossetti, called for high windows in the nave and double windows in the chapels, thereby ensuring diffused and congenial lighting. In the presbytery area, on the other hand, the deep choir is flooded with light providing a strong contrast with the darkness of the triumphal arch and the windowless dome.

The lower order that frames the chapels, and the upper one that serves to punctuate the bays of the nave, have the effect of breaking up the wall while providing a simple yet sophisticated decoration.

The handling of the façade is also of considerable interest. Here large pilasters are used to accent the large module and small arches decorated with terracotta to stress their internal sections. The same decorative motif is used again on the campanile, which was rebuilt only a few decades ago.

San Cristoforo alla Certosa. *1. Side portico and Church; Entrance avenue to the Church; 3. Entrance Shrine to the side portico; 4. Side cloister.*

or several years the church has been closed
 restoration and it will doubtless be imposs-
e to visit it properly arrayed with its works
 art in the near future. For the time being,
se are kept in the city's museums. Under the
sent circumstances, it will suffice to mention
t Bastianino, Bastarolo, Niccolò Roselli and
er late sixteenth-century artists produced
ntings for this church.

his large church is now situated in a charm-
 setting which, notwithstanding the construc-
n of the monumental cemetery, begun in 1813
lowing a plan by Ferdinando Canonici, can-

3

not have changed all that much since the time of the Estes. The church dominates the open green area that stretches as far as the city wall. Visitors sensitive to the unique atmosphere of Ferrara should make sure they visit a little-known corner that lets you view the church in all its inspiring splendour. You should make your way to Via delle Vigne (the last section of Via Montebello) and, at the entrance to the Jewish cemetery, turn left down the unpaved road. From this vantage point, among the cultivated fields and tumble-down walls, one can gain a surprising view of the Carthusian monastery, farm-houses, the Jewish cemetery, the last unspoilt corner of 16th — century Ferrara — the natural and urban landscapes join in a seapless continuum.

THE MASSARI PARK AND PALACE

As well as the Palace itself and its various annexes, the Massari grounds also boast a large public park, landscaped in the mid-nineteenth century in Romantic style, and still well - appointed with a splendid flora.

The Palace was erected towards the end of the sixteenth century by the Bevilacqua family, who continued to change and modify the

ilding throughout the centuries that follow-
. In the nineteenth century the new owners,
e dukes of Massari, further embellished the
ilding. As a result, the interior now contains
iccoes, and frescoed ceilings and a variety of
corations from the beginning of the seven-
enth to the end of the nineteenth century.
erall, the palace interior, even if it is not
presentative of the era of the Este family's
eatest splendor, provides nonetheless a good
ample of a noble residence, in which changes
d additions made at different times coexist in
rmony.

The Civic Museum of Modern Art is now bas-
in the buildings attached to the Palace, which
so house other temporary activities related to
e museum. In particular, the piano nobile is
ven over to a collection of the most significant
neteenth — and twentieth — century Fer-
rese painters, including Filippo de Pisis. On
e ground floor there is a documentary section
«metaphysical painting», covering the main

stages in the history of this great artistic movement. Special attention is paid to De Chirico
whose works are reproduced in a series of colour slides, since the originals are scattered all
over the globe.

Also in the so — called Palazzina dei Cavalieri
di Malta («Palace of the Knights of Malta»),
there is an exhibition of nineteenth — century
artists, including approximately 150 works by
Giovanni Boldini (1842-1931).

n Cristoforo alla Certosa. *1. Graveyard; 2. Tomb of Bor-*
3. Tomb of Borso: interior.
Corso Porta Mare. Massari Palace.
Massari Park.

PIAZZA ARIOSTEA

We have already considered the role played by this square as a gravitational pole within the Ercole Addition. However, it is worth taking a closer look at various other aspects of Rossetti's plan.

Since this is the «new» square, the most significant piece of open space in the whole of the Addition, the visitor naturally expects it to be encircled with important landmark buildings. Surprisingly, however, the square is instead a green area overlooked by simple, and in some ways distinctly «popular», buildings.

The only ones worthy of note are the **Palazzo Rondinelli** and the **Strozzi-Bevilacqua buildings**. In both these Rossetti used the portico, are element in the local tradition, as a ways of «filtering» the transition between the empty outside space and the construction itself. Rossetti's very special sensitivity, his awareness of the function of buildings in the broader city context, is eloquently demonstrated by the way the porticoes are aligned with the streets that lead into the square. It is worth taking a careful look at the Strozzi-Bevilacqua portico. As can be seen, this constitutes a point of encounter (and mediation) between present-day Via Palestro and Via Borso, leading to the Carthu-

sian monastery.

The present-day appearance of the squa[re] dates back to roughly 1930. The late nineteen[th] century statue of Ludovico Ariosto now stan[ds] in the place of other earlier statues (of Po[pe] Alexander III, of Liberty, and of Napoleo[n]) which have taken their turns in line wi[th] political developments.

1. *Massari Palace: a hall of the «piano nobile».*
2. *Piazza Ariostea during the Palio of St. George.*
3. *Piazza Ariostea, in the background Rondinelli Palace*
4. *Bevilacqua Palace.*

VIA MONTEBELLO

On the street of the Ercole Addition that still keep to the original layout, the most significant — apart of course from Corso Ercole I d'Este — is certainly Via Montebello. To form an idea of the city that Rossetti had envisaged, with its expansive and spacious aspect, its rectilinear plan, and its grandly aristocratic but umpompous buildings, this is the street that demands attention. Even if this environmental characteristic has been partially disfigured by the asphalt pavements that have been laid, Via Montebello should nonetheless be visited thoroughly in order to experience the succession of ther sobre-fronted buildings, churches and convents.

At the crossroads where Via Montebello and Via dei Prioni (now known as Corso Porta Mare) meet stands the Church of **Saint John the Baptist**. Work on this building began with the apse area, following a design by Biagio Rossetti, and was continued by Girolamo da Carpi and Schiatti.

Because of the appalling conditions into which the church has fallen, it can no longer be visited. One can note, however, its compact and imposing mass and the dome that enables one to spot this church, among the others, from afar.

Of the other buildings, the **Santo Spirito** monastery merits particular attention. This complex is dominated by the huge mass of the church itself which overlooks a churchyard that until a few years ago was much larger. Its late sixteenth-century cloister, currently being restored, is notable for its configuration, which is wholly untypical of Ferrara. Indeed, this cloister has a high portico with large brickwork pilasters that accentuate the breadth of space surrounding the monumental stone well.

VIA MORTARA

Via Mortara is another important straight stretch of street in Rossetti's city design. Here used to stand two large convent complexes, both at present undergoing restoration.

The first, **Santa Maria delle Grazie**, erected at the beginning of the sixteenth century and seriously damaged by events over the centuries, has unfortunately lost a cloister. Of the church itself, only the outer shell has remained. The surviving cloister is an example of simple architecture, with two levels of balconies in brickwork.

The second, **Santa Maria della Consolazione**, is yet another complex designed by Biagio Rossetti and located at a «strategic» point in the city, on the corner of Via dei Prioni and Via Mortara, the last main road going eastwards. The church was not completed until

after the death of Rossetti. One can recogi Rossetti's hand, however, not so much in tempts at the vertical and horizontal parti that may be seen in the unfinished façade in the apse and the interior. The apse, bellished with pilaster strips on the outs floods the presbytery with light through its h side windows. The nave and two aisles, the per order design, and the windows, all re previous churches, in particular San Cristof

The convent with its cloister and faç overlooking Corso Porta Mare is also of inter These buildings date from the end of the ei eenth century, when the complex was used an orphanage.

PALAZZO NASELLI-CRISPI

Planned by Girolamo da Carpi in appr mately 1530, this building is absolutely uni in Ferrara. One may appreciate, especiall the courtyard, the classical scheme derived f examples of Roman architecture which, w congenial to Girolamo, gained little follow among most Ferrarese architects. Indeed, other building may be found in the city in wl the use of the overlaid architectural order is c ceived, as is here, with such up-to-c references to classical architecture.

The very recent restoration of this buile has reasserted the contrast between

brickwork and the imitation stone of the order, highlighting the elegance of the composition.

In the brickwork façades with alternating triangular and elliptical tympana windows, we find a prototype which, adjusted to suit local tastes, enjoyed a certain popularity throughout the second half of the sixteenth century.

CHIESA DEL GESÙ

Planned in around 1570, this church, even though it was subsequently remodelled, has preserved in the layout of its façade the typical forms of late sixteenth-century Ferrarese architecture. This façade was, it appears, the work of Alberto Schiatti. Inside, among the other works of art, the famous Mortorio, made by Guido Mazzoni in 1485, stands out.

Against the polychrome terracotta background, human figures writhing in a torment that is expressed with a sort of violent despair, surround the dead Christ. In the figures' contorted faces, the artist's reference to the conventional mime of popular theatre is apparent, as are the echoes of Tura's dramatic sensibility. On the right-hand side among these figures, Duke Ercole I and Duchess Eleonora of Aragon may be seen, who, in this sacred representation, portray Joseph of Arimathea and Mary of Cleophas.

Via Montebello; 2. The Church of S. Giovanni facing the lls and the Israelite graveyard; 3. Via Borgo Leoni. Naselli-ispi Palace; 4. Naselli-Crispi Palace, view of the recently ored courtyard; 5. Piazza T. Tasso. Church of Gesù.

AN BENEDETTO

his large Benedictine complex, begun at the
of the fifteenth century, has unfortunately
n severely damaged over the centuries,
ecially during the bombardments of the Se-
d World War. As a result, the church that
v stands is an almost total reconstruction,
dly undertaken between 1952 and 1953, of
one built by Rossetti. The cold appearance
he resulting building, due to the roughness
he new material, creates an unfavourable ef-
t, and makes one wonder whether complete
onstruction is always fully justified. It should
, however, be forgotten that the church, and
ecially the flank that overlooks the street,
yed a role within the overall scheme of par-
lar landmarks in the «Ercole Addition»,
ich was of such fundamental and essential

importance. Therefore, however much it may
be an «architectural forgery», the visitor is
recommended to enter this church and to devote
some thought to this space and to Rossetti.

As is the case with the churches of Saint Francis and of Santa Maria in Vado, here too the
Renaissance scheme of composition is evident.
The interior in fact consists of an aggregation
of the square base modules, used in the bays of
the nave, transept and apse. The modules of the
aisles and chapels are only half as long and
broad as the base module. This means that the
quantity of chapels is, as it were, automatically
determined. This follows the plan of the two
churches previously mentioned. Here, however,
the concatenation of geometrical elements is
rigorous even in the transept and apse, where
the central dome is encircled by three exactly
identical modular spaces. The resulting area is
at once compact and outlined with effective
clarity.

As with San Francesco, the aisles are lit from
the windows located to the sides of the chapels.
The semicircular shape of the chapels, inspired
by the work of Brunelleschi, help to diffuse the
light, thereby softening the dramatic *chiaro-
scuro* of the Franciscan church.

Of the decorations that survived the church's
collapse under bombardment during the Second

rch of Gesù. *1. Interior; 2. «Mortorio»; 3. Corso Porta
St. Benedict's Church.*

World War, one should note the «f[...] evangelists» of the nave pendentives, the w[...] of Ludovico Settevecchi (sixteenth century[...]

On the way out of the church, one may pa[...] to admire the campanile built by Giovan B[...] tista Aleotti. Ever since it was erected in 16[...] this slender and simple tower has been one [...] the most significant urban landmarks of the «[...] cole Addition», playing a role similar to that [...] the castle towers and the campanile of [...] church of Saint George.

Many sections of the huge several-cloister[...] monastery — another victim of wartime bo[...] bardment — have been lost, and many of th[...] parts that remain are now encircled by squa[...] post-war constructions.

Two cloisters that still possess a number[...] decorated rooms may still be visited — e[...] though they are in a very poor state of rep[...]

St. Benedict's Church. *1. Bell tower and apse; 2. Cloi[...] 3. Via Ariosto. Ludovico Ariosto's house.*

HE HOUSE OF UDOVICO ARIOSTO

‹Parva sed apta mihi; sed nulli obnoxia sed n sordida; parta meo sed tamen aere domus». This sentence, engraved on the cornice sums the relation of perfect symbiosis existing beeen the house and its owner, the poet Ariosto. iving reached his mature years, Ariosto dered the house to be built, perhaps to a sign by Girolamo da Carpi, in order to thdraw there to compose the final draft of his *lando Furioso*. The sentence in Latin exesses his view of the house: «Small but suited me... and made with my own money», but also reveals the poet's reserved character and the pride he felt in his moral and material freedom. The sober sixteenth-century front (to which his son, Virgilio, had a plate added, that reads: «Sic domus haec Areosta propitios deos habeat olim ut pindarica»), the distribution of the spaces inside the house, the wooden floors, the small courtyard, still today emanate a tranquil and meditative atmosphere. It was the image of a house as refuge, simple and dignified. The grounds included a large vegetable garden, that occupied the poet's free time. This building, which was purchased by the Municipality of Ferrara in the mid - eighteenth century, is now used as a branch library for the district.

THE CITY WALLS

The tour of the fortified circle of walls is a still largely unknown excursion tour in Ferrara. It is however to be recommended not only for its intrinsic historical interest, in terms of military architecture, but also for the beauty of the landscape, most striking and enjoyable on the northern and eastern sides of the city. It is unthinkable that any tourist who has appreciated the mediaeval city and admired the broad streets of the «Herculean Addition» should complete his, tour of the Ferrara of the Este Family before experiencing the rarefied and almost timeless atmosphere of the city walls.

The layout of the whole structure, built over a time-span of approximately two centuries, has survived almost unscathed. Most of the ramparts can be visited as can large stretches of the embankment even though parts of the walls (the Pontifical fortress, the bastion of San Rocco, the gates of Saint Benedict, Saint George, Saint John, and others) were demolished from the 17th century onwards. These features make the city walls the largest and most suggestive park in Ferrara, a delightful blend of history and nature.

The lenghty time span that was required to complete the definitive structure of the city walls, renovating them and adapting them step by step to the requirements of defence, has resulted in a certain typological variation between different sections. This can be seen most clearly if one compares the section built by Rossetti and the southern bastions of Alfonso II. Despite this variation, the whole of the Ferrara circle of walls may be classified as an example of what historians term the «Italian-style bastioned front».

Before launching into a more detailed description of the walls, it should be emphasized that the city's defences until mediaeval times con-

sisted essentially of very high but relatively th battlement walls, interrupted by towers th were usually square, and encircled by a mo. This pattern, basically unchanged until the f teenth century, underwent a radical alterati when firearms became so powerful that th constituted a serious threat to the very stat ity of the walls, which being high were all t more easily pierced and demolished.

From the last decades of the fifteenth centu onwards, walls were therefore built lower. T outer sloped curtains (stretches of wall betwe towers) were reinforced on the inside by ve thick ramparts designed to serve as bulwark on the outside the moat and more raised ra parts assured further protection. A fundame tal element in this system was the bulwark bastion, consisting of an advance block plac before the wall curtain. Initially, these bulwar were circular in cross-section, but later assu ed the more «classical» pentagonal or «ace spades» form.

The function of the bastion was to interru the curtain sections, in such a way as to prese to the enemy a surface that was not straigl thus causing their gunshot to be deflected. Tl accounts for the variety of forms assumed I the bastions, never situated parallel to the wal The bastions also lodged at their top the artille emplacements, and in their sides the so-call «traitor pieces»: from these could be fired fla shots skimming the curtain walls, therel defending their straight sections.

The whole course of development affectii later types of the bastion is represented in tl city walls of Ferrara, from the most rudime tary form of turret known as the «Torrione d Barco» (built in approximately 1492) to the mo elaborate bastion built by Alfonso II (post 1560

The Rossetti Walls. In chronological orde leaving aside the very few sections remainii of the Borso wall to the south, all of which we radically altered after 1560, one finds the wal of the Herculean Addition, which encircle in a almost trapezoidal form (from the present-da Porta Po to Corso Giovecca) the late fifteent century expansion of the city.

Under the direction of Biagio Rosset assisted by Alessandro Biondo, the city, havii abandoned the old circle that ran along the li of the present-day Corso Giovecca, was suppli with walls with a «modern design» after 149 The section of the quadrilateral that is certai ly the work of Rossetti runs from the Torrior del Barco (north-west vertex) to the Gate Saint John (the Gate to the Sea). This is certai

one of the most striking stretches of the wall, well as being of a most singular design: it has loping wall curtain, a bastion detached from e wall, and small round turrets. The whole nstruction is surrounded by a large green ea, retracing the perimeter of the original oat. Focal points include the circular topped lwarks, of which the north-eastern one, own as the «Duke's rotunda», no longer exs, and the gates: the one known as the Gate

Angels, situated approximately half-way und the northern side, traditionally held to ve been closed off after the exodus of the Este mily and their followers from the city (1598), d the Gate of Saint John, of which only the eat circular turret remains.

Many parts of the curtain walls in this secon were rebuilt during the course of the eighenth century, and a number of intermediate nall turrets have disappeared. Rossetti's sign has not however been substantially tered by the changes, and not even the largeale destruction that long decades of abandonent have wrought on the wall surfaces has sucesses eded in destroying the significance of the

133

walls as a primary example of «a bastioned front».

If one follows the ramparts one cannot help but be struck by the harmonious relation existing between the city walls and the surrounding territory, whether one looks out into the countryside (towards the Duke's Bark-once the private hunting ground of the Este family), or towards the city itself where one can still espy broad stretches of free land, the eighteenth-century Jewish cemetery, and the Certosa buildings: a series of delightful and charming vistas.

The Walls of Alfonso I. From the Gate of Saint John, towards the south, run the more typically fifteenth-century walls with steeper scarp-backed ramparts. The first section, as far as the Gate of Saint George (no longer extant),

was built by Alfonso I between 1512 and 15 Among other interesting features, there are triangular bulwark of Saint Thomas, and bulwark «of the Mountain». The latter deriv its name from the large earth embankme created to form a cavalier, i.e. a raised artille position. From the edge of this bulwark one c admire the «Ducal Baths», attributed Girolamo da Carpi.

In this section, as in that further to the nor the bed of the ancient moat can still be trac in precise relation to the walls. By contrast, the area adjacent to the former Gate of Sa George (now the city's exit in the direction Ravenna), this relation has been wholly lost a result of the numerous constructions that ha been erected on the ramparts.

The Walls of Alfonso II. The last constru tions that the Este family undertook in order extend the city's fortifications were the southe bastions. Remaining still intact is the sequen of those bastions built in order to reinforce t «Borso» walls (proceeding clockwise: t Bulwark of Love, of Saint Anthony and of Sai Peter). These bastions, built on the initiative the last Duke, Alfonso II, in approximate 1580, are splendid examples of a defensive a that had by this time reached maturity. Indee they were provided with technical featur which for those times were very modern: the «ace of spades», i.e. recessed star shape; t

ecial postings for raking fire; their internal
rvice and manoeuvre rooms; and their sum-
t artillery emplacements.

Whereas the structures are on the whole quite
ell preserved, the embankment and rampart
ve been tampered with in recent times. This
tracts from the overall interest of the area.
The remaining part of the walls may still be
sited, but has lost forever those features that
ake the aforementioned sections famous. The
st faint trace of the transformations effected
the Papal Government of the early seven-
enth century, following the destruction of the
ighty fortress in the mid-nineteenth century,

The Certosa and the Israelite Graveyard seen from the walls;
Part of the walls and embattled tower of Porta San Giovan-
3. Walls and bulwark of San Tommaso; 4. Walls of Borso
l Bulwark of Buon Amore; 5. 18th-century sentry-box of
bulwark of the Mountain, last left among the so many which
ved as guard-posts along the walls; 6. Porta Romana; 7. Porta
ola.

is the Paola Gate, erected in 1612 by Gian Battista Aleotti as a monumental approach from
Bologna.

The imposing papal fortress, which was
finished in 1610, was demolished in the 1800s.
This loss weakened the city's defenses as it had
been one of the key elements, with its five-point
star plan and complex layout of bastions, ramparts and ditches. The last two remaining bastions are Santa Maria and San Paolo.

SAINT GEORGE

During the period of Este rule, the Saint George group of buildings of Olivetan monks was a fully-fledged active and self-sufficient village, including a church, three interconnected cloisters, and a series of other secondary buildings. Unfortunately, the architectural distribution of this structure, similar to that of numerous other Benedictine communities, is now seriously impaired. Still standing, however, even if modified, are the church, the campanile, and the first cloister — which the friars still use to this day. As for the other parts of the complex, one can gain an idea by entering, off to the side of the building, the village. On the right-hand side stand the scant remains of the service buildings, once used as storehouses, cellars, workshops, etc. And, at the bottom of the lane, stands a building showing clear vestiges of the third cloister. All these buildings were turned into houses several decades ago.

Right down the centuries, however, the fate of Saint George seems to have been to alternate

between splendor and decadence, mutilatio and restorations.

Ferrara's first episcopal seat (from the 7 century), Saint George nonetheless declin rapidly following the consecration of the n cathedral of Saint George in 1135. Having l its previous importance, the village was us less, and as a result its primitive architectu structures fell into such a state of disrepair th when Nicolò III d'Este granted San Giorgio the Olivetans in 1417, they had to rebuild bo church and convent.

The fact that Biagio Rossetti, from 1473 o

...ok a hand in the work of renovating this ...uster of buildings is borne out in documentary ...vidence. Due to the subsequent alterations, ...owever, Rossetti's architectural contribution ...an only be identified at a very few points: the ...acristy, the layout of the first cloister, and the ...ampanile. It is worth taking a careful look at ...e campanile before going in. Its function in ...e broader context of the village is evident: it ...erves as a landmark for those leaving the city ...s well as for those seeking to approach it from ...e surrounding contryside. This is all the more ...riking if one recalls that until the beginning ...f the fifteenth century the convent stood in ...tal isolation, without any other buildings near ... When it came to drawing up a plan, Rossetti ...ust have born in mind not only the examples ...rovided by local mediaeval architecture, but ...lso the cathedral campanile then under con- ...truction. Reference to the cathedral is in fact ...pparent in the division of the tower body into ...quare blocks. On the other hand, rather than ...eproduce the vigorous sculptural style that

Piazzale San Giorgio. Set of St. George's Church; 2. Bell ...ver of San Giorgio del Borgo; 3. Detail of the façade. St. ...orge kills the dragon, bas-relief; 4. Bell tower.

137

Alberti had adopted for the cathedral (a manner fundamentally foreign to Ferrara), Rosse
ti opted for a smooth arrangement of surfac
that were relieved or «patterned» by means
angular pilaster strips and decorated cornice
a «meeting point» between old and new, a com
mon feature in Rossetti's architecture.

Of the fifteenth-century church, for whi
Cosmè Tura painted the Roverella (1475) an
the Saint Maurelio (1479) altar-pieces (both
which have been lost), not much is left. The pr
sent façade was reconstructed in the first ha
of the eighteenth century, set further back tha
the original one. The interior, rearranged
1581 by Alberto Schiatti, was later decorate
by seventeenth-century artists including, mo
notably, Francesco Ferrari.

Inside the church one can visit the famou
tomb of Lorenzo Roverella, a Ferrarese bisho
(1475). The complex architectural an
sculptural design of this work is attributed
Antonio Rossellino, who also made the lunet
depicting the Virgin Mary and the angels an
sculpted the five statues of saints in the niche
The other parts of the tomb were the work
Ambrogio da Milano. Overall, the elegance
the composition of this tomb and the fir
balance of the forms make it a landmark
fifteenth-century Emilian sculpture.

The three silver plates (1512) adorning the
on the sepulchre of Saint Maurelio (chapel
he left of the apse) are also of outstanding
stic quality. They represent: Duke Alfonso
neeling before Saint Maurelio; Duchess
rezia Borgia, followed by five ladies, presen-
her firstborn Ercole to Saint Maurelio; and
Prior of the Olivetans of Saint George kneel-
before the Saint. The Ducal family probably
mmissioned this work from Giovanni Antonio
Foligno as a way of giving thanks for the vic-
y at Ravenna, in which Duke Alfonso had
ned distinction alongside the Ferrarese ar-
ry. The final plate is of special interest. In
background are depicted the city walls and
church of Saint George: one can see quite
inctly the tiered orders of the campanile, as
l as the façade with its Venetian style up-
half.

George's Church. *1. Cloister; 2. Interior; 3. Funeral monu-*
t of Lorenzo Roverella; 4. Apse concha; 5. St. George vic-
us.

THE DELTA DEL PO

CASTLE OF MESOLA

The small town of Mesola is situated on the banks of the Delta's southern branch, the *Po di Goro*, where it is crossed by the ancient Romea Road.

The town clusters around the castle which, with its four-turreted bulk, dominates both it and the surrounding countryside. The castle is immediately visible on approaching the small town along the avenue of poplars that one turns onto from the Via Romea.

Commissioned by Marchese Alfonso II d'Este, the Castle of Mesola was built beween 1579 and 1583 as a hunting residence set in a vast reserve. Architect Giovan Battista Aleotti worked to a design by Marcantonio Pasi.

The building, on a square plan without an inner courtyard and with four battlemented towers positioned transversally at its corne was constructed on three floors. Following long period of abandonment, it has recen been renovated and converted for use as cultural centre.

The outer courtyard is surrounded by l buildings which once served as servan quarters, stables, warehouses, and for other p poses related to everyday life in the cast Nowadays several of these buildings are us as shops, public offices, and craft worksho

The Grande «Delizia» remained in the poss sion of the Este family until 1785 when it w purchased by Pope Pius VI along with t «Woods of Mesola», a large reserve bounded the Po di Goro, the Po di Volano and the se

ˈOODS OF MESOLA

These woods (part of which may be visited
  Sundays and Bank Holidays) have now
:ome a great natural reserve with a surface
:a of over 1,000 hectares. This safeguards
ˈt of a forest that once covered much of the
ꞮVINCE. The rich flora of this area is domi-
ed by the holm oak.
Ɬhe fauna is as plentiful and varied as its flora
Ɪ includes: deer, fallow-deer, hares, badgers,
Ɪ otters.

ꞯUTHERN PO DELTA

Ɪ picture of the natural environment of the
  Delta may be completed by pressing on fur-
ꞮR towards Goro and Gorino, following the
ꞮKS of the Po di Goro, into contryside where
Ɪ principal element is water.

The whole area was once marshy, and all that
could be seen were cane-brakes and the occasional fishing-hut. The prevalent activity was
fishing, and the technique used was that of the
«*lavoriere*» — net traps set in swamp ponds,
«fenced off» by islands of reeds.

Land reclamation has transformed broad
areas of the marshes into cultivable land. From
the banks and spits of land, where canals divide
into myriad branches and lose themselves in the
sea between the reed beds, one can still admire
a rare natural environment of water, sand, and
rushes.

---

*1. Castello Estense of Mesola; 2. A fine specimen of Deer in
Mesola's Wood.
On page 142-143. Views of Goro, Gorino and the Basilica of
Pomposa.*

141

THE ABBEY OF POMPOSA

The Abbey of Pomposa was founded about the 7th century on the Island of Pomposia, an area bound on two sides by branches of the Po in its delta — the Po di Goro and the Po di Volano — and on the third side by the sea.

At the time of the Abbey's foundation the area, though isolated by the surrounding marshes of the delta, enjoyed a healthy climate and abundant woodland, factors which encouraged the settlement of the Benedictine community and its subsequent expansion.

In the High Middle Ages the Abbey was a nucleus of culture, exerting both religious and civil power over a vast area. The prestige and prosperity of the Abbey continued unabated until environmental changes turned the area into marshland, rendering it first inhospitable and finally uninhabitable. The monks began to leave the island for the Monastery of San Benedetto in Ferrara in the early 16th century, finally abandoning it altogether in 1671.

Some of the monastic buildings have today disappeared, but the parts which remain are of inestimable architectural and artistic value. The **church** as it stands today dates from the 11th century, the period in which the **bell-tower** (1603) and the atrium — the work of the architect Mazulo — were added to the original, simple basilica. The decorations on the walls are rare examples of great interest: maiolica bowls of Byzantine origin, cornices and friezes in tw coloured terracotta with plant and anim motifs, and sculptures with symbolic figure

The inside of the church was complete frescoed in the 14th century by artists of t Bologna school and includes work by Vitale, t school's founder. The frescoes in the nave p tray Old and New Testament scenes, wh those of the arches show scenes from t Apocalypse; on the inside of the façade the L Judgement and in the apse the glorified Chr with the Angels and the Saints.

The decorated floor is divided into thr parts. The section in the Presbytery is a mos dating from the 5th century in the style of t Ravenna masters; the inlaid marble work of t central section (11th century) with its geomet design reveals Venetian-Byzantine influen and contains, in the centre of the square, t eight-pointed star of Pomposa; the third secti with its figures of animals also dates from t 11th century.

The walls of the **Chapter House** a decorated with frescoes of the Rimini scho (early 14th century).

In the **refectory** the frescoes, dating fro the second decade of the 1300's, portray t supper of San Guido, Christ with the Madon and the saints and the Last Supper; these, to are attributed to artists of the Rimini scho

The **Palazzo della ragione** (Palace Justice) today offers the visitor an unlike perspective in its double loggia, the result o

newhat over-imaginative restoration project
our own century; it was from this Palace,
merly connected to other buildings of the
nplex, that the Abbot dispensed justice and
ninistrered the affairs of the population.

'rom the right aisle of the church the visitor
reach the **Museum of Pomposa** with its
uable collection of sculptures, frescoes and
haeological exhibits connected with the Ab-
r's history.

lica of Pomposa: *1. Interior; 2. View of the cloister and
ctory's façade; 3. Fragment of a frieze in Greek marble
esenting a griffin (end of the 10th cent.) preserved in the
lica Museum.*

3

145

COMACCHIO AND ITS «VALLI»

HISTORICAL SKETCH

The earliest historical evidence regarding Comacchio dates back to the 8th century A.D. The image that emerges is that of a wealthy lagoon town surrounded by marshes (known as «Valli», with a harbour linked to what was then the largest channel of the Po. The town's economy was sustained by a mighty fishing fleet as well as by a thriving trade in sea salt—of which Comacchio was the major source in the north of Italy.

The breach of Ficarolo in 1152, after which the main channel of the Po shifted nortwards, the ill-fated war with Venice (9th century), and the misgovernment under first the Este family and subsequently the papacy, all contributed to Comacchio's steady commercial decline.

In the seventeenth century, the town's rulers became interested in the marsh fishing trade, and also turned their attention to the town's architecture an land reclamation.

This recovery culminated with the Napoleonic treaty of 1797, which formally stated that the «Valli» belonged to the people of Comacchio. This acknowledgement was repeated in 1868 by the Kingdom of Italy, with regard to the C[...] mune of Comacchio.

The reclamation of the «Valli», which the [...] family had initiated in the seventeenth centu[...] progressively reduced their surface area f[...] 1865 onwards. The Trebba, Ponti, and I[...] «valli» were drained early on, but the proc[...] continued right into the 1950s and 1960s [...] the reclamation of Pega, Rillo, Zavolea [...] Mezzano. In their place, farming has been [...] troduced.

COMACCHIO

The present layout and architecture of [...] town date back to the second half of the 1[...] century. There is a principal road axis runn[...] from East (Church of Saint Maurus and S[...] Augustine) to West (Church of Saint Mar[...] «Aula Regia»). This is crossed by six waterw[...] spanned by brickwork bridges.

The town's buildings, their fronts overl[...] ing the canals, are arranged in rows separa[...] by alleys from which a series of narrow la[...] spread out like the teeth of a comb.

In the southern part of the town the *Trep*[...]

146

erally: «Three Bridges») (1634) and the
idge *degli Sbirri* (literally: «of the cops»), both
signed by the architect Luca Danesi, are
nong the most beautiful features of Comac-
io's typically lagoon architecture. Situated in
e same area are the seventeenth-century Fish-
arket, the eighteenth-century former Saint
millus Hospital, designed by the architect
schini, and the Bellini Palace, an aristocratic
ilding constructed in 1865 now used as a
useum and cultural centre.

The most important buildings in the city cen-
are: the Merchants' Loggia, built in 1621,
ancient granary; the Clock Tower, a
neteenth-century reconstruction of an earlier
venteenth-century tower; and the Church of

Aerial view of Comacchio.
The Three Bridges (Trepponti).
The clock tower seen from Via Edgardo Fogli.

147

1. Church of Carmine (17th cent.) and «Pizzetti» bridge
2. Bellini Palace.
3. Loggia of the Merchants with the bell tower and
Cathedral in the background.
4. The 17th-century Ponte degli Sbirri and behind the clas
lines of the façade of the ex S. Camillo's Hospital.

148

e Rosary erected in 1618, which houses six-
enth - and seventeenth - century art works.
Proceeding westwards from the centre one
counters the cathedral, built in 1659 to a
sign by the architect Cerutti on the site where
e Chiesa Madre di San Cassiano had been
ected in 708 AD.
In linear baroque style, the cathedral contains
statue of Santa Lucia in white marble with
lychrome traces, dating from the first half of

the fifteenth century, eighteenth-century works
of art.
Further to the west one comes upon a baroque arcade, known as the *loggiato* «of the
Capuchins», built in 1647, and consisting of 152
arches. This is situated alongside the Church
of Saint Mary in «Aula Regia», erected in the
seventeenth century, which houses a Crucifixion by Giuseppe Mazzuoli (known as «il
Bastarolo»).

THE «VALLI»

Comacchio is surrounded by «Valli», a large lagoonal area of over 9600 hectares, offering a wide range of exciting views and a natural environment rich in aquatic and bird life. This area of marshes is famous not only for its many rare migratory and non-migratory birds, but also for its extremely numerous eels which spend several years in its mirky depths before returning to the Sargasso Sea spawning grounds.

1 and 2. Views of the marshes; 3. Eels; 4. Fish-screen system.

SPINA

In 1922 and 1952, inside the lagoonal are two vast Greco-Etruscan necropolises we brought to light. Then, in 1956, the town Spina, dating back to the 6th century B.C., v discovered in the «Valle» of Mezzano.

1. Palafitte.
2. Red-figured Kelebe.
3. Red-figured Lekytoi.
4. Volano beach.

The excavations, which are still proceeding Spina, and the finds unearthed from the cropolises, which are now kept at the national useum of Spina in Ferrara, afford us an inresting glimpse of the city and culture of this cient lagoon port, which disappeared in the rd century B.C.

THE BEACHES

Ranged along Comacchio's sea coast, on the far side of the Via Romea — itself an ancient boundary between marshland and the sea — lie seven beaches or «Lidi», bathing resorts well-equipped to welcome visitors and holi-daymakers. From south to north one may visit: «Lido di Spina»; «Lido degli Estensi»; Porto Garibaldi, a harbour at the mouth of the canal linking Comacchio to the sea; «Lido degli Scacchi»; «Lido di Pomposa»; «Lido delle Nazioni»; and «Lido di Volano», only a few kilometres from the Abbey of Pomposa.

CENTO

The history. The town of Cento, located 35 [ki]lometres away from Ferrara, projecting [to]wards the cities of Modena and Bologna, on [th]e banks of the Reno river, represents an im[po]rtant historical, artistical, cultural and [ec]onomic episode in the province. Of uncertain [R]oman origin, the first documents dealing with [th]e town date back to 799, and here Casale Cen[to] is mentioned as a boundary of a territory own[ed] by Nonantola Abbey.

At the end of the 12th century the town con[si]sted of a quadrilateral protected by a moat, [wi]th four entrance gates and divided into four [qu]arters, under the domination of the Bishops [of] Bologna.

In 1502 Cento became part of the Este ter[ri]tory, as a dowry granted to Lucrezia Borgia [by] her father, Pope Alexander VI.

Once the irregular course of the Reno river [w]as kept under control by turning it into a [tr]ibutary of the Po near Ferrara, and once the [la]nds north of the town were reclaimed, Cento [be]came a flourishing territory, economically [bo]und to the production of hemp.

Such a growth was largely due to the peculiar [ol]d system of «participations» according to which the territories were periodically allotted in collective properties that ensured welfare and development to the population, and to the political authorities the recovery and control over marshy territories often flooded by the Reno.

Cento thus always enjoyed a certain autonomy and special privileges in duties, in the control of the waters and in arts.

After a relevant growth not only in the economic, but also in the literary, scientific and cultural field, Cento was eventually allowed to

1. Porto Garibaldi; 2. Holiday camps on the Lidi; 3. Cento: Piazza del Guercino with Town Hall (17th cent.) and Governor's or Clock Palace (16th cent.).

155

become a «city» by Papal bull of Benedict X on December 18th 1754. Many a persona historians, men of letters, philosophe mathematicians testify the cultural liveliness this centre, from Alberto Accarisio (1497-15 who wrote the first dictionary of the Ital language, to the historian Girolamo Baruffa (1675-1755); but among all stands out distinguished painter Gianfrancesco Barbi called «Guercino» (1591-1666), a true leading tist: many of his works are still left in the tov

The centre of the town. The town is s well legible in its 14th-century layout.

At the crossing of the two main streets, wh connect the old gates of the town, is the squa On to it stand the battlemented Governc Palace with the clock tower (1502, rebuilt in early years of this century) and the 17th-centu Town Hall.

Down the main streets, characterized by typical arcading system, are placed palaces a churches of remarkable historical and archit tural value.

The most important among the churches San Biagio's which, more than once rebu dates back to 1045; in its baroque interior i possible to admire the choir and a canvas Guercino representing «Christ giving the k

St. Peter». Some other churches are to be
mentioned, the romanesque St. Peter's, the
church of the Rosary, designed by Guercino,
and the Church of the Servants: these two have
both works by Guercino inside.

Among the palaces we mention Rusconi
Palace, Pannini House, along the arcades of
Corso Guercino, with the characteristic wooden
structures, Provenzali House, the Borgatti
Theatre; just outside the girdle of walls stands
the Rocca, rebuilt in 1460 on a former fortifica-
tion of 1378.

_Casa Pannini probably built in the first half of the 15th
century with the characteristic wood-trabeated portico on wooden
pillars; 2. Via del Guercino. The Municipal theatre and, in
background to the right, the City Hall; 3. The fortress, second half of the 15th century; 4. Municipal Theatre (1856-61).
Central part of the façade slightly jutting out, decorated with
red and yellow polychrome strips and with a rich terracotta ornamentation; 5. Guercino (and collaborators), « The Virgin of
Carmelo gives the scapular to S. Simone Stok and Saints», Central Picture Gallery; 6. Porta Pieve, probably built towards the
end of the 14th century._

FERRARA

Legend:

① Castello Estense
② Cathedral and Cathedral Museum
③ City Hall
④ St. Dominic's Church
⑤ St. Paul's Church
⑥ Palazzo Paradiso and seat of the Ariostea Municipal Library
⑦ St. Francis's Church
⑧ Palazzo Estense S. Francesco called of Renata di Francia and seat of the University
⑨ Casa Romei
⑩ Church of S. Maria in Vado
⑪ Palazzo Schifanoia
⑫ Palace of Ludovico il Moro and seat of the Archaeological Museum of Spina
⑬ Biagio Rossetti's House
⑭ Church of S. Antonio in Polesine
⑮ Church of S. Carlo
⑯ Palazzo Roverella
⑰ Church of S. Maria dei Teatini
⑱ Palazzina of Marfisa d'Este
⑲ Arcispedale S. Anna
⑳ Palazzo Turchi di Bagno
㉑ Palace of Diamonds and seat of the National Picture Gallery
㉒ Palazzo Prosperi Sacrati
㉓ S. Cristoforo alla Certosa
㉔ Palazzo Massari and seat of the municipal Museum of Modern Art
㉕ Palazzo Bevilacqua
㉖ Piazza Ariostea
㉗ Palazzo Rondinelli
㉘ Church of S. Giovanni Battista
㉙ Israelite Graveyard
㉚ Church of Gesù
㉛ Church of S. Benedetto
㉜ Ludovico Ariosto's House

Articles

- The medieval town
- The town of the Renaissance
- The walls
- Saint George

by CARLA DI FRANCESCO

- Historical background
- Downtown Ferrara
- The Po Delta
- Comacchio and the hills
- Cento

by MARCO BORELLA

Editorial and graphic coordinating
Federico Frassinetti

Photographic feature by Ascanio Ascani from Misano - Forlì
Other photographs by: Civica Fototeca of Palazzo Schifanoia,
Foto G.R.A. - Roma, Foto Marco Caselli - Ferrara,
Federico Frassinetti, Alceo Marino, Mario Rebeschini,
Paolo Zappaterra, Foto A. Scapin
Civica Biblioteca del Comune di Cento.

Printed
by La FOTOMETALGRAFICA EMILIANA SPA
San Lazzaro di Savena - Bologna

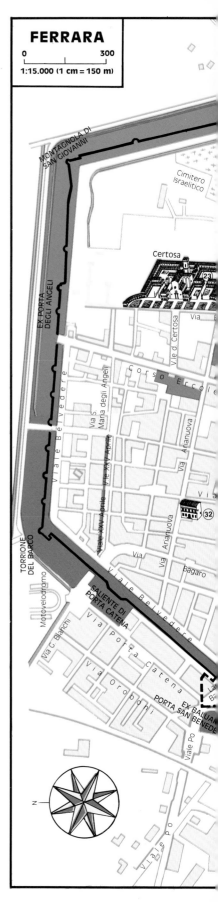

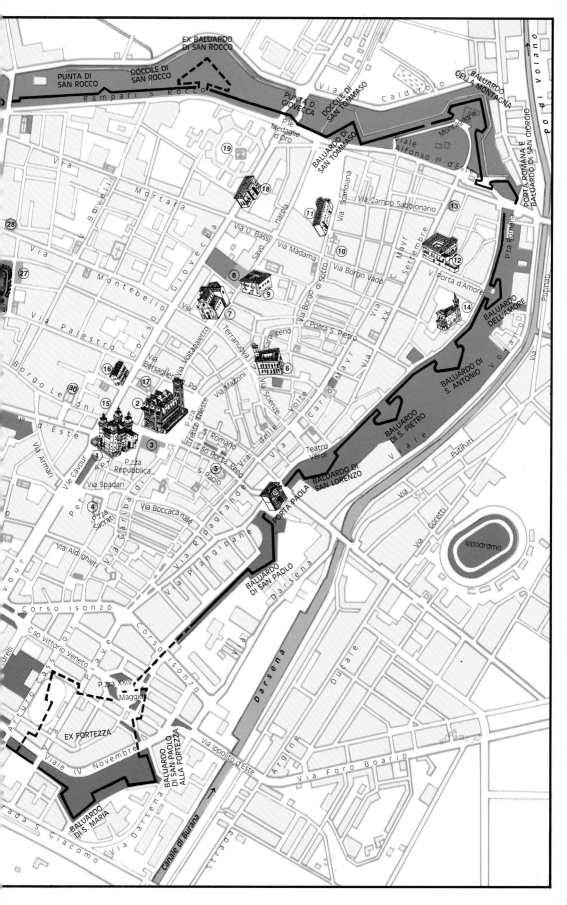

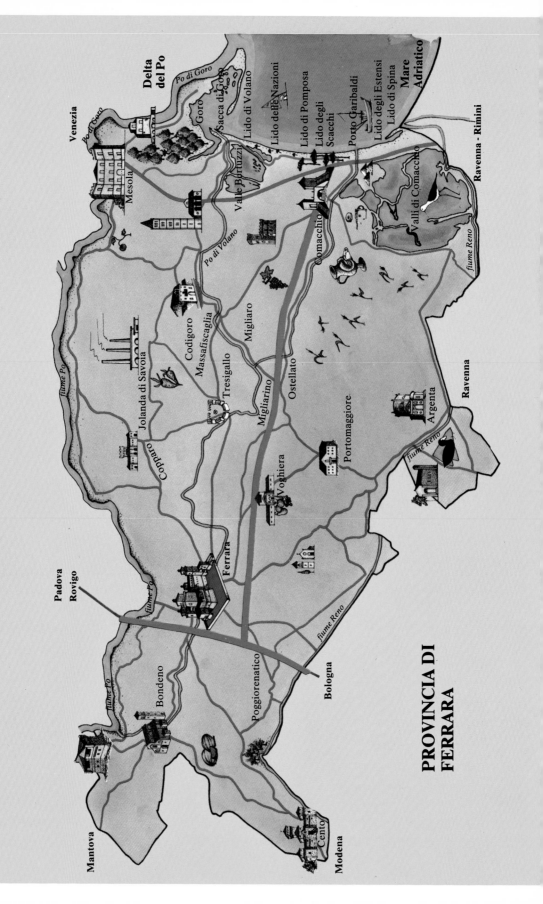

PROVINCIA DI
FERRARA